THE HUMANISTIC COACH

THE HUMANISTIC COACH

From Theory to Practice

BENNETT J. LOMBARDO, ED.D.

Professor and Chairman

*Department of Health, Physical Education,
Recreation and Dance*

Rhode Island College

Providence, Rhode Island

CHARLES C THOMAS • PUBLISHER
Springfield • Illinois • U.S.A.

Published and Distributed Throughout the World by
CHARLES C THOMAS • PUBLISHER
2600 South First Street
Springfield, Illinois 62794-9265

© *1987 by* CHARLES C THOMAS • PUBLISHER
ISBN 0-398-05326-X
Library of Congress Catalog Card Number: 87-1866

With THOMAS BOOKS *careful attention is given to all details of manufacturing and
design. It is the Publisher's desire to present books that are satisfactory as to their physical
qualities and artistic possibilities and appropriate for their particular use.* THOMAS
BOOKS *will be true to those laws of quality that assure a good name and good will.*

Printed in the United States of America
Q-R-3

Library of Congress Cataloging in Publication Data

Lombardo, Bennett J. (Bennett John)
    The humanistic coach.

    Bibliography: p.
    Includes index.
    1. Coaching (Athletics) I. Title
GV711.L64   1987   796'.07'7   87-1866
ISBN 0-398-05326-X

To my coaches:
Mom, Dad, Angela, John, Susan,
and John Cheffers

PREFACE

THIS BOOK challenges virtually all aspects of current practice in athletic coaching. It is the author's intention to stimulate those in athletic coaching to carefully analyze present assumptions, and re-examine most of what coaches and athletes accept regarding their roles, purposes, and functions as leaders and participants within the sport setting.

At all levels of sport one readily observes approaches employed which hinder significant learning, if not rendering it impossible. This takes place not because of some inner depravity that coaches possess but because they, in most cases, are not aware of feasible alternatives. There are alternatives. This book has been designed to present suggestions for change to those currently involved in sport and athletic coaching within the context of educational systems.

The focus of all human movement programs, including sport and athletics, is people. Therefore, the emphasis throughout is on the individual. In recognition of the athlete-centeredness of the coaching task and the problems usually encountered when individuals attempt to translate humanism into prescriptions for behavior and effective practice, I have titled this book *The Humanistic Coach: From Theory to Practice*.

I have placed the athlete at the center of this work and have attempted to demonstrate that athletic coaching is concerned with much more than the organization and management of groups of people. The focus, instead, is on how participants in athletics are affected by adult leadership and coaching behavior.

The book puts forth the idea that athletics within organizations purporting to contribute to the growth and development of the participant should be enjoyable as well as promote learning. Indeed, the athletic endeavor will be increasingly more significant and be more directly beneficial to the individual if it is humanistic.

The author does not pretend to have all the answers. In fact, concepts, theories, and activities will be presented with which the reader will take issue. If this does take place, then I shall have achieved one of my purposes in commiting these thoughts to paper. My hope, however, is to move coaches to reflect on athletics and sport in a different manner and, at the very least, come to a clearer understanding of an approach to athletic coaching and sport which centers on the person within the experience and which embraces the concept of humanism. If this occurs, then my efforts must be deemed fruitful.

In Part I of Chapter 1, the reader is presented with a description of the writer's assumptions regarding the sport experience. This section attempts to elucidate such beliefs, with the goal of minimizing misinterpretations, and possibly enhancing the clarity of the thoughts outlined in later sections.

The second part of Chapter 1 outlines and reviews the commonly proposed and commonly accepted outcomes of the athletic experience. Specifically, the psychomotor, social, cognitive, affective, physiological, etc., results of the sport experience are identified. These suggested outcomes are reviewed in an attempt to develop commonly accepted expectations from participation in sport.

In Chapter 2, I have provided a brief overview of the two most pervasive and competing theories of psychological thought: psychoanalysis and behaviorism. This was done in an attempt to provide background information to those not familiar with the major forces in psychology.

Chapter 3 discusses the potential effects and benefits of the humanistic sport experience on all those directly involved in such an endeavor. Specifically, the potential outcomes that will accrue from structuring sport humanistically and fostering humanistic coaching behavior are examined. Each of the three parts focuses on one of the three major aspects of the sport experience: sport in general, the coach, and the athlete.

In Chapter 4, humanistic theory is translated into practice. Specific examples of humanistic coaching behavior are presented and emphasized in this section. The initial section reviews the present state of coaching, devoid as it is of humanistic coaching models, both in theory and in actuality. Covered also is an analysis of why such humanistic models are not prevalent within sport. Next are presented some hints on how to get started moving athletic leadership, and sport in general, towards humanism. Two scenarios follow that are presented to clarify the notion of humanism in sport. The scenarios present a holistic view of sport and coaching behavior, so that the reader can visualize how one might specifically organize sport, behave as a coach, and what to expect from athletes. The final part of this chapter presents specific examples of humanistic coaching behavior, along with the intent and possible contribution of such behavior to sport and athletes.

Chapter 5 recapitulates and summarizes the major themes presented in this work. It also addresses the future and attempts to identify the next stage of development in the progression to humanistic sport. Included in this part is the identification of a few suggestions for change in the system of sport directed at a broader administrative level.

It should be clear from all of this that changes at levels above the coach-athlete, coach-team level are called for. Changes of a structural nature are required to improve the sport experience, in general, and these changes should take place concurrently with specific changes in coaching behavior.

The goal of this work has been to strike a unique and singular balance between a review of humanism and an application of this perspective to a relatively unexplored and unattended area.

CONTENTS

THE HUMANISTIC COACH

Chapter 1

THE GOALS
OF THE SPORT EXPERIENCE

PART I: ASSUMPTIONS

PRIOR TO the delineation of a proposal intended as an alternative to the current system of sport, an examination of beliefs fundamental to such a system is in order. In other words, what are those aspects of the sport experience that the writer takes for granted? It should be noted that many of these assumptions can be found among the written records and material of many adult-sponsored athletic organizations.

1. The Voluntary Nature of Sport.

It is assumed that participants come to the competitive sport experience of their own choosing. The participants are there because they want to be there. Individuals are not coerced into participating or joining. By the same token, athletes are able to leave the experience of their own free will. Indeed, the mass exodus of athletes across the land that predictably takes place annually in many organizations has stimulated many treatises which have addressed this phenomenon in an attempt to explain and possibly resolve it to the satisfaction of all concerned.

2. The Particular Sport Has a Strong Intrinsic Appeal for the Participant.

Initially, the athlete enters the activity because he/she enjoys it. Enjoyment is the primary motive for participation. The individual, for whatever personal reasons, discovered that he/she has fun doing this activity, be it swimming, soccer, or baseball, and believes that the adult-sponsored organization can serve as a vehicle for maximizing this enjoyment.

3. All Participants Develop in Many Ways and at Many Levels as a Result of the Sport Experience, Regardless of the Specific Manner in Which the Program Is Administered.

Athletes learn about themselves, others, and their world as a result of their involvement with sport. The athletes will learn verbally and nonverbally. They will develop physiologically and psychologically. This growth and development will accrue as a result of direct contact with people and encounters with various situations, regardless of the exact form that the behavior of the coach or the organization takes. Interaction of the athlete with the environment always brings about change (i.e. learning). It is safe to state that an endeavor so meaningful and so profound to so many will lead to many important, albeit often personal, discoveries.

It is not suggested, however, that all participants discover and/or learn the same things. The exact and specific nature of the revelations and learnings will vary, paralleling the variation and uniqueness of each participant and reflecting the individual's personal encounter with sport.

4. The Adult-Sponsored Sport Program Has an Educational Intent.

The organization is desirous of contributing in a positive manner to the growth of the athlete. In many such groups these purposes are formally codified and publicly displayed and promoted. These serve to guide the leaders within the organization. In other less formal programs, this belief is at least included in the rhetoric of the organization. Minimally, organizations include reference to such objectives in the rhetoric of the program. Increased motor proficiency, physical development, and strategic sport knowledge are areas that most programs would anticipate at least minimal growth. Other, more idealistic groups might possibly focus on and actively promote the goals of social relationships, moral integrity, sportsmanship, respect for others, etc., as additional valuable outcomes.

5. Athletes Possess a Great Variety of Reasons for Entering the Sport Experience, All of Which Are Meaningful and Relevant to Them and Include, But Are Not Limited to, Increased Motor Proficiency and Winning.

Participants come to the sport experience seeking and anticipating the attainment of various objectives, which are relevant to them. Enjoyment was mentioned previously as the initial and primary motivator for entrance into the formally organized activity. Over and above this goal, athletes have many reasons for joining, not all of which relate to achieving victory or enhancement of motor skills. Moreover, many of the motives of the athletes are not congruent with those of the adult leader. It is quite possible that other objectives may be more potent for the participant than winning, such as playing, action, recognition, comradery, social relationships, etc. Griffin (1978) reported that athletes valued such objectives as learning the game, conditioning, and forming friendships. Sapp and Haubensticker (1978), Gill, Gross, and Huddleston (1981), and Gould et al. (1982) all reveal that fun, affiliation, the demonstration of power, the pursuit of excellence, and the experience of thrills or excitement are valued by athletes. The literature not only indicates that athletes have several, often diverse motives for participation but also that winning may be more highly rated by, and more important to, the adult in the formal sport program.

PART II: THE CONTRIBUTIONS OF THE SPORT EXPERIENCE TO THE GROWTH AND DEVELOPMENT OF THE INDIVIDUAL

There appears to be general support for the view that sport is an institution of modern society which has considerable importance. The institution of sport, reflecting as it does society's beliefs, values, and norms, has the potential to significantly influence participants. People become involved in athletic programs because of the assumed potential contributions of such an experience.

It is important, then, to review the potential benefits and the possible outcomes which are often attributed to participation in sport. The reader should be cognizant of the fact that these outcomes should ideally accrue from the athlete's encounter with sport. Unfortunately, in too many cases, this is not so. This latter phenomenon has provided partial impetus for this book.

It should be kept in mind that most of the contributions described herein, although often included in goal statements and other promotional materials of many athletic organizations, are not necessarily addressed directly in sport programs as presently conducted. Actual behavior is often incongruent with formally avowed goals. Instead, efforts are all too often concentrated on those goals thought to be more closely related to winning and motor proficiency.

Attainment of these outcomes are not automatically guaranteed simply because the individual enters the sport program. The effects of athletic programs vary greatly, dependent mainly upon the specific athletic leadership provided. Some outcomes are achieved regardless of the specific management of the athletic program (e.g. the athlete's confrontation with the stress of competition, the emotional control of anxiety, and the athlete's encounter with personal success and failure). In some cases, the goal must be attended to in a direct manner by the athletic leadership or the goal will not be attained (e.g. the development of the physiological component of cardiovascular efficiency in baseball; a cognitive understanding of the strategic reasons underlying the hit-and-run play). Moreover, there is an irregular and disparate pattern of development and/or attainment of such goals, dependent upon the specific patterns of participation of the athlete (e.g. how much time the individual actually practiced, performed in actual competition, and sat on the bench watching).

This section attempts to delineate the various contributions to individual growth that participation in sport can make and to provide the reader with the background against which the goals and potential contributions of the humanistic model, as proposed in this text, can be measured. At a later time, this section should facilitate the determination of how, in what ways, and to what extent the humanization of sport can contribute to the individual involved. In addition, the reader will be able to ascertain if humanized sport contributes to the athlete in the same way and to the same degree as the pervasive, traditionally structured sport organizations.

How does participation in sport contribute to the growth and development of the athlete? What are the goals of the encounter with sport? What do advocates and supporters of participation in sport claim to be the major contributions and significant outcomes of such an encounter?

PHYSICAL. As a result of involvement in sport, it is anticipated that the individual's physiological status will be improved. Participation in sport can be helpful in the development of physical fitness. Sports participants may improve in one or more of the components of physical fitness as they strive to improve their performance in the particular sport. Physical fitness will be enhanced, at least temporarily (i.e. for the duration of the specific sport season). Indeed, this might be the most often-cited rationale for participation in sporting activities.

It is assumed that the physical capabilities of the athlete will be improved. Improved strength, muscular endurance, flexibility, cardiovascular efficiency, and neuromuscular functioning are expected outcomes of regular participation in sport activities.

Participation in sport should serve as a vehicle by which athletes discover the boundaries of their physical capabilities and their physical being. Minimally, even if physical development does not result, athletes should encounter their bodies in a number of ways not usually experienced in daily pursuits. Sport provides opportunities to feel and observe the body working in stressful situations. In many ways this fosters self-awareness and self-understanding.

Participation in sport should result in improved motor performance. In conjunction with, and building upon, the improved physiological status of the performer, there should result a heightened efficiency of the athlete's motor performance. Timing, power, agility, accuracy, etc., should all be enhanced, resulting in better performance. Kinesthetic awareness will be improved, leading to a subsequent gradual decrease in the variability between performances. That is, the athlete should demonstrate higher levels of skill in the activities that are regularly practiced. Motor behavior and motor performance should, in general, be enhanced and the individual should become more proficient at the tasks practiced.

An additional consequence of sports participation relates to future motor skill acquisition. The regular instruction, the multitude of practice sessions, corrective feedback about performance, conditioning programs, etc., should facilitate the acquisition of motor skills and enhance the individual's future motor behavior and performance. The sport experience, in effect, makes the individual more ready to learn, participate in, and perform motor activities in the future.

Finally, mention must be made of the potential long-term effects that involvement with sport might have. Mager (1973) suggests that leaders in educational contexts must maintain or improve the participant's interest for the subject at hand, be it academic, sports-related, or whatever. The worst possible outcome of any learning experience would be a decrease in the participant's interest in the activity. Siedentop (1983) refers to such interest as an approach tendency, defined as "any behavior . . . that would allow one to conclude that they find the subject and the learning experience satisfying, enjoyable, valuable, interesting, challenging. . . ." (p. 22). Repeatability is a term often used to express this phenomenon. Simply stated, a fine sport experience, assuming it has enhanced the athletes' approach tendency to sport and the physical aspects of it, enhances the possibility that athletes, at a later date and hopefully throughout their entire lifetime, will repeat the activity. Eventually, with continued, repeated participation, athletes may come to value such activity so highly as to include it as a vital part of their lifestyle.

An excellent sport program can have this effect. It can make the sport encounter so enjoyable that athletes will come to value physical activity in a way that it will insure their physical vitality for many, many years.

COGNITIVE. Minimally, the athlete should learn the rules, strategies, tactics, and skills of the sport. The individual's understanding of the specific cognitive and mental aspects of the sport should be broadened. In addition, an understanding of the intricacies of the components of each motor skill in the sport should result.

The athlete should learn the "why" (i.e. rationale, reasons) underlying each phase of the sport. The level of thinking on behalf of the athlete should require higher levels of cognitive functioning (i.e. evaluation, analysis, synthesis), rather than emphasize rote memorization. In addition, meaningful decision-making opportunities, inherent in all sports, often require critical, creative, and imaginative thinking abilities. It seems logical, then, to emphasize in the instructional component provided within the sport program the processes involved in such high-level, conceptual work. Consequently, these qualities of cognition should be expected outcomes of the sport experience.

Another aspect of cognitive development which authorities in sport feel should be emphasized in the experience of sport is the encouragement of divergent thinking (Boyle, 1963; Luschen, 1967). The term "change agent" has been employed to identify this potential benefit of the sport encounter (Wilkerson & Dodder, 1979). By this term, authorities suggest that the encounter with sport can serve as a vehicle for societal change. Since sport allows for participation, and therefore interaction between all levels of society and all peoples, its effects can be wide-ranging and it can stimulate change which could have considerable effects. Add to this the current widespread visibility afforded sport via the various media outlets and the potential for influencing and initiating change in society appears quite powerful.

Self-evaluation, introspection, and self-analysis are other forms of intellectual activity which should characterize encounters with sport. Athletes should be encouraged to think critically and creatively about their performances; to do so will foster the growth of their mental and intellectual capacities. Opportunities for self-analysis and self-evaluation are pervasive within the athletic context. Indeed, such situations are a critical, vital part of the sport experience, whether or not the athletic leadership chooses to direct attention to them or not.

Participation in sport can and should facilitate the athlete's ability to concentrate, which can heighten the participant's performance in other aspects of daily living. Concentration is the ability to keep the mind focused on the present activity, the here and now. The ability to block out everything but the present subject of attention transfers very well to a multitude of important tasks of life.

PSYCHOLOGICAL. There are several important outcomes that should result in this area. It is important for athletes to discover their capabilities, their limitations, their strengths, and weaknesses, all of which will lead to a better understanding of self. Numerous opportunities for such learnings related to self-discovery exist in sport. As a result, the encounter with sport can assist in the process of self-acceptance by providing experiences which foster self-discovery and understanding of self.

Participants in sport have a multitude of opportunities to experience success. The phenomenon of a successful (however one defines success) sports career is assumed to be translated and carried over into other aspects of daily living. The recognition, validation, and confirmation of an individual's worthiness, which can accrue from ventures into sport, can become a continual source of satisfaction, pride, and self-esteem.

Well-designed sport programs structure the athletic experience in such a way as to maximize the individual's success. In other words, sport programs which contribute the most to its participants ensure that each athlete is validated, confirmed as a worthy person, and is successful.

Participation in sport often becomes a source of self-esteem and thereby can contribute to the development of a strong, vital self-concept. The athlete should increase his/her self-confidence. If success in sport is defined as the completion of the tasks involved in participation in sport (e.g. preparation, training, planning, competing, self-evaluation, etc.) rather than the more limited, albeit more popular definition of conquering the opposition, then success is well within the grasp of all competitors. Increased self-confidence should result if the athlete experiences success (as defined previously) in his/her motor activities. The satisfaction thereby derived from successfully harnessing the capabilities of the mind and body to achieve a level of motor proficiency, as well as the completion of a complex task, should result in social approval as well as reinforcing the individual's intrinsic motivation. This phenomenon should foster positive self-feelings and, thereby, an enhanced self-concept.

Experienced athletes are often assumed to be more assertive, if for no other reason than the sport experience continually places the athlete in competitive situations. The athlete who remains in sport must become comfortable with competition and must develop a modicum of assertiveness (if not aggressiveness) in order to survive the often tough, cruel arena which is sport. Social evaluation, continual comparisons with others, and repeated self- and team analyses require that the athlete not only develop a "thick skin" but also be able to deal with such anxiety on a regular basis. If an athlete cannot do this, the individual will usually drop out of the sport. It is for these reasons that many feel that the individual who has had extensive sport experience can deal with competitive situations and, it is argued, bring such abilities, experiences, and traits (i.e. competitiveness) to other aspects of daily living.

Self-discipline is often a direct result of participation in sport. The ability to take charge of one's life, to make decisions relevant to one's world, and then to carry out such decisions leads to positive psychological growth. The commitment to sport, which often entails an explicit promise to attend all meetings, practices, and games, places the burden of responsibility on the athlete. Often, quite a bit of personal, social, and familial sacrifice is required. Adherence to training regimes often mandates self-denial on behalf of the participant. The experience of establishing a team goal and generating plans and activities designed to facilitate the attainment of this goal requires the athlete to employ time-management skills and long-range planning. In short, the sport experience often results in the development of self-discipline, which in turn often leads to intrinsically motivated individuals, at least those for whom sport remains attractive (i.e. those who do not drop out). Such individuals have learned how to manage and take control of their own lives and are often (or become) very independent individuals.

Sport can foster the development of self-direction and often enhanced levels of intrinsic motivation. Improvement in ability can then be attributed to the individual's efforts, rather than the result of efforts external to the athlete. In this case, the individual will take pride in his/her accomplishments. The feeling of being confident and competent will develop, possibly leading to a more self-efficacious individual. Bressan (1982) believes that:

> As individuals achieve increasing degrees of skill in motor performance, a general feeling of environmental coping may expand toward feelings of real competence and belief in their ability to act effectively in response to challenging situations. The learning of sport . . . enables an individual to

engage in controlled movement settings where physical performance becomes concrete evidence upon which to base self-evaluation. . . ." (Pp. 20-21)

The motivation to achieve and to be competent quite possibly develops into a characteristic of the individual as a direct result of the sport experience.

It is expected that the athlete will be able to control his/her emotions better as a result of the sport experience. Encounters with rules, officials, opposing players, and fans (both supportive and non-supportive) requires a measure of emotional strength and control. The experience of striving for limited rewards, working with his/her team against another group, within the context of rule-invoking referees and partial onlookers displaying abilities in public, eliciting often harsh, realistic, severe social evaluation demands a modicum of emotional stability and control. The performers, at some point, must develop the ability to manage their reactions to the arousal and resulting stress that is ever-present in sporting events.

The athlete must learn to modulate and adapt his/her emotions and feelings related to the occurrence of victory and defeat. More importantly, the athlete must develop a level of emotional balance that enhances, rather than detracts from, motor performance. That is, athletes have to learn to control their arousal and anxiety level in order to maximize their performance.

The experience of sport can also contribute to the emotional development of the athlete, if it is structured in such a way that the performer is permitted to express his/her enjoyment and excitement related to the sporting event. Encouragement of such emotional expressions or release will support athletes in their efforts to express and discover their inner beings.

Sport furnishes the participants with unique opportunities for non-serious exploration with their universe. Sport should emphasize its playful aspects so as to focus more attention on its non-serious nature and the unlimited potential for experimentation and exploration which it presents to the athlete.

The outcomes of sport should result in a state of pleasure, satisfaction, and enjoyment, bringing the performer joy that is surpassed by few other activities.

SOCIOLOGICAL. Involvement in sport contributes greatly to the socialization process. Sport is a very effective socializing agent for those who identify with and value it. The encounter with sport can socialize such predisposed individuals into the prevailing normative order and value patterns of the adult society that he/she is about to enter. In effect, the experience of sport can significantly effect the process to enculturate the individual into society. As a reinforcer of culture, the sport experience can facilitate the integration of the individual into society.

Responsibility to others and commitment to group goals are often confronted directly for the first time in the sport situation. It is often during the competitive experience that individuals become aware of their responsibility to others as well as the need to focus clearly on both short-term and long-range objectives. Being part of a team or group committed to sport requires the filling of specialized roles and following through on many duties, both of which can nurture the individual to greater social awareness, sensitivity to others, and responsiveness.

Wilkerson and Dodder (1979) point out that through sport experiences, which present "opportunities for vibrant emotional expression of individual and human qualities" (pp. 50-51), the individual can affirm his/her identity. In an attempt to resist and combat the forces of homogenization, impersonalization, and bureaucratization in society, sport can and should provide opportunities for individuals to express themselves, to proclaim their uniqueness and subjectivity, and to provide evidence that individuals know themselves.

Sport can be a vehicle which can facilitate the development of several positive social variables so important, according to Wilkerson and Dodder, at a time when in our complex society so many people experience great difficulty establishing meaningful contact and maintaining ties with others (1979). Participation in sport can be a major force in the development of such aspects as: (1) the ability to get along with others, (2) cooperation, (3) the ability to compete in a socially approved manner, (4) comradeship, (5) social interaction and communication skills, and (6) satisfaction of affiliative needs.

AFFECTIVE. It should be noted that an encounter with sport should result in an increase in the individual's interest in the activity. Using Mager's (1973) terminology, the athlete's "approach tendencies" toward the sport should be enhanced so that the desire to repeat the activity remains strong. Certainly, a good sport experience would minimally strive to insure that the participants feel good about, enjoy, and obtain some sense of satisfaction from the activity, all of which would reinforce the athlete's interest in repeating the experience. Well-designed athletic programs attend closely to maintaining and strengthening such approach tendencies.

Another ramification of the development of enhanced affection for the specific sport relates to the potential for long-term life-style enhancement. It is quite possible that increased affection for the sport could lead to the inclusion of physical activity in the form of participation in sport or other forms of physical activities, which in turn will positively enhance the individual's physical being. The effects on the individual's life-style would certainly be beneficial.

Chapter 2

AN OVERVIEW
OF HUMANISTIC PSYCHOLOGY

PART I: WHAT IS HUMANISTIC PSYCHOLOGY?

HUMANISTIC psychology is a perspective of mankind and human behavior comprised of two major themes: (1) man's essential wholeness and (2) man's unfulfilled potential. The emergence of humanistic psychology was spurred by the efforts of several significant individuals (e.g. Coombs, Jourard, Perls, Rogers, Maslow). The major impetus for humanism was provided by the conscious efforts made by its originators to formulate a functional, yet optimistic view of humanity. Their efforts were aimed at the development of a third psychological movement which would markedly contrast with psychoanalysis and behaviorism. Both of these latter schools of thought set forth a pessimistic notion of man and his development.

Both behavioral scientists and psychoanalysts are "committed to the assumption of a deterministic universe" (Jourard, 1968, p. 227). Psychoanalytic psychology, dominated by the Freudian tradition, assumes that humans are driven by impulses derived from biological needs of their bodies. "According to the psychoanalytic view, man, while he can be free (or freer), is mostly a vessel driven by instinctual urges and irrational super-ego prodding" (Jourard, 1968, pp. 104-105). Consequently, man strives to satisfy these needs and to reduce tension and frustration. Psychoanalysis also emphasizes the interplay between unconscious emotional forces and the conscious organization of human behavior, despite the fact that unconscious forces cannot be experienced directly (Maslow, cited in Roberts, 1975). According to Maslow, psychoanalytic psychology "has confronted . . . the nature of man. But . . . these have been handled by being very cynical about them, . . . by analyzing them away in a pessimistic, reductive manner" (Roberts, p. 305).

Behaviorism, on the other hand, emphasizes the control of man via the environment. Man is conceived of as a passive reactor to the environment. Behavioralists suggest that man can be shaped in any direction, manipulated by external forces in such a manner that future behavior can be confidently predicted and controlled. Behavioralists also refuse to deal with human consciousness because it cannot be systematically and objectively studied. Therefore, human subjectivity, introspection, and consciousness are not included within the framework of behaviorism. In this view, then, there is an inherent determinism regarding human behavior, coinciding with a denial of man's individual cognitive capacity and his free will.

Moreover, Maslow (1962) points out that until recently "psychology has most studied not-having rather than having, striving rather than fulfillment, frustration rather than gratification, seeking for joy rather than having attained joy, trying to get there rather than being there" (p. 69). This pre-occupation with the deficiency model of man precluded the development of a psychology based on healthy, fully functioning individuals.

Humanistic psychology (sometimes referred to as the "third force" in psychology, with psychoanalysis and behaviorism being the first two), however, is quite different. It rejects both the Freudian notion that the personality is ruled by unconscious forces and the behavioristic idea that individuals are wholly controlled by their environment. Rather, humanism is optimistic in its view of mankind. It insists that man has untapped potential to positively take control of his life and, because of potentially unlimited cognitive capacity and his personal autonomy, can avoid the inevitable external manipulation as explicitly described by behavioral scientists.

Jourard (1968) succinctly summarizes the essence of humanistic psychology. He explains that:

> A humanistic psychologist . . . is concerned to identify factors that affects man's experience and action; but his aim is not to render the man predictable to, and controlled by, somebody else. Rather his aim is to understand how determining variables function in order that a man might be liberated from their impact as he pursues his own free projects. (P. 18)

Humanism suggests that all individuals have these capabilities, although these potentials often go unfulfilled. Humanists emphasize the importance of man's free will and his inherent human ability to make choices. However, in contrast to existential thought, which focuses on the uselessness of life and a general pessimism, humanistic psychology defines life as a positive growing experience, emphasizing the individual's ability to enhance his/her awareness via direct experience with the world and to strive consciously and continually for self-actualization. Lastly, humanistic psychology includes within its framework and attaches great significance to psychological needs, such as love, self-esteem, belonging, self-expression and creativity, which are often excluded or dismissed as being too ephemeral, too difficult to study or account for by both psychoanalytic and behavioral psychologists. These latter needs are described by humanists as among those which truly define the unique character of man, exposing in fact yet another major difference between humanism and the other two schools of psychology.

PART II: THE BASIC TENETS OF HUMANISTIC PSYCHOLOGY

At this time it would be appropriate to briefly summarize the main tenets of humanistic psychology.

1. A Major Thrust of Humanistic Psychology Is the Great Importance Placed on the Personal and Subjective Interpretation of Human Experience.

Each individual brings to each setting a unique personal history and a unique perceptual system, both of which color his/her interpretation of the experience of the moment. Therefore, each individual has a legitimate right to his/her own unique feelings, views, interpretations, perceptions, etc. These singular and unique interpretations are based upon the individual's perception of his/her conscious experience. Inherent in this view is the strong belief in the concept of freedom of the individual.

2. Man and His Experience Are Viewed Holistically.

Humanistic psychology insists on viewing man as a total functioning being, not as many discrete elements. Humanism refuses to view man as equal to any one part or to the sum of his/her parts. Rather, humanistic psychology goes beyond this view and insists that each individual, in a uniquely human manner, adds to such parts (e.g. traits, mind, body, brain) a particularly individual humane dynamism, which in part accounts for the uniqueness and the singular character of each being.

Humanism does not concentrate upon a particular part, element, or physiological structure in its efforts to understand human behavior.

Contrast this concept with the behavioral focus on man's observable behavior and man's dependence on the environment and external stimuli. Similarly, the psychoanalytic approach emphasizes the subconscious, past experiences, and inner drives. Humanistic psychology insists that man experiences each of life's activities with his/her entire being, mind, body, and soul subjectively behaving as one, integral, whole person (Maslow, 1970). Humanistic psychology, for example, would insist that when studying mathematics an individual experiences the subject matter as a multidimensional, yet unified whole person, not limited in response to mental processes or restricted solely to affective interpretations. The person's entire body is simultaneously and directly experiencing that lesson. Likewise, in the movement setting, man experiences the activity at many levels—physically (e.g. muscular effort, increased heart and breathing rates), cognitively (e.g. understanding the consequences of movement; the relationship to others, to objects; where to move, how to move), and affectively (e.g. enjoyment of or dislike for the activity, fear, or anxiety). Humanistic psychology, with its emphasis on increasing awareness, growth, and change, suggests that it is foolhardy to separate, discrete phenomena of our consciousness. Humanism does not deny the simultaneous "experiencing" that the person undergoes.

3. The Concept of Freedom and Autonomy Is Central to Humanism.

It is a distinctly human characteristic to be able to overtly behave one way while covertly "acting" (i.e. thinking) in the exact opposite manner. The humanistic perspective is one which attempts to harmonize the individual's sense of autonomy and the theoretical model that it sets forth (Shaffer, 1978).

Individuals make many choices daily, including the decision to deny their personal autonomy and freedom. An essential part of the human experience is our ability and need to make decisions. Humanism refuses to accept the behavioral notion that people are passive reactors, unable to behave in any way other than that which is elicited via the stimuli in the environment and reinforcement patterns (Shaffer, 1978).

4. Humanistic Psychology Is Anti-Reductionistic in Its Orientation.

Experience is not analyzed into component parts. Attempts are not made to generalize from many discrete experiences to one unifying construct. Direct experiences with the world are viewed as "genuine phenomena" and are not rationalized as "manifestations of . . . drives or as reflections of early states of need-satisfaction" (Shaffer, 1978, p. 16). Rather, special attention is directed to increasing awareness and utilization of consciousness to enhance one's experience and growth. Again, humanism centers on the person's interpretation and respects the individual's view, rather than attempting to analyze and reduce all experience to more basic drives or psychological defenses. The subjective experience is celebrated and respected for what it is, rather than for objective, comparative or analytical reasons.

5. *There Is the Belief That Human Nature Can Never Fully Be Defined.*

Since reality is viewed as being personalized and subjective rather than objectively given, it is impossible for one person to truly know the experience of another. If, therefore, experience and reality are individually defined and human nature consists of human behavior, there results a problem of objectively analyzing human experience. Shaffer (1978) states: "If the limits of human nature are not certain, then the human personality is infinitely expandable" (p. 17). Consequently, humanism insists upon emphasizing the concept of man perpetually striving to know, to understand, to become fully aware of, and to become fully conscious of him/herself in order to better understand human nature as best we can. Yet, the humanist stops short of generalizing one individual's experience to another.

Since human nature can never fully be defined, it must continually be actively pursued. Each person must strive to know him/herself. Humanism, therefore, sets forth the view of man's endless, but self-revealing, struggle for completeness, for self-actualization, and to realize his/her unfulfilled potential. Here, humanism is truly unique in its positive and optimistic belief in mankind. Man, autonomous and free, struggles throughout a lifetime for self-enhancement. This uniquely optimistic and positive conception of mankind, striving for and motivated by an innate desire to grow, to improve, to achieve, and to be competent, contrasts with the motives ascribed to man by psychoanalysts (i.e. tension-reduction) and behaviorialists (i.e. reward-seeking). Humanists subscribe to the notion that this optimistic view of mankind accounts for many human behaviors which have puzzled psychologists for years (e.g. self-sacrifice, altruistic behavior, delayed gratification). Mankind is in a perpetual process of "becoming" and growing throughout life. This point of view sharply contrasts with the concept central to the Freudian tradition, that is, man's continual need to reduce tension, to minimize frustration, and to gratify his/her desires.

Chapter 3

THE POTENTIAL OF THE
HUMANISTIC SPORT EXPERIENCE

PART I: HUMANISM IN SPORT:
THE MISSING ALTERNATIVE

THIS SECTION investigates the reasons for the absence of humanistic coaching models in both the sports establishment and the professional literature on sport. Where are the alternatives to conventional programs? Where are the humanistic programs? Where are the humanistic coaches? Why does there appear to be such a dearth of humanistic athletic leadership? The writer is confident that such programs and individuals exist, but locating and identifying them has proved difficult.

Coaches, as well as athletes, parents, and spectators, have, by and large, simply not paid much attention to humanistic approaches to sport. Humanism is flippantly dismissed as impossible, implausible, or inappropriate in terms of the current, real world (i.e. the professional model) of sport. At the present time, organized sport encourages mindless conformism and a sense of pessimism related to the possibilities for (creative) play in the sport setting.

Another factor which inhibits the emergence of truly humanistic athletic programs relates to the mismatch between the formally expressed goals of the organization and the informal, actual behavior of the leaders and administrators commonly observed in amateur sport. Many sport programs limit their effectiveness in many ways, including their efforts at humanizing their organization, because of their efforts to equate and accommodate the goals and methods of sport designed to have an educational or recreational impact with those of professional athletics and its commercial-business orientation.

Moriarty, Guilmette and Ragab (1977) outline the extent such discrepancies between belief and actions occur in amateur sport in their case-study report. Data from a written opinionnaire of 1,400 parents and players indicated that socialization, fun, and the pursuit of excellence should be the functions of Little League baseball. Yet, game observations indicated that the behavior of all involved was centered on winning, perfecting technical skills, and other product outcomes, all of which minimized efforts at maximizing social interaction, the development of personal relationships, and enjoyment. Their results indicated that there exists in sport today a conflict between the goals of sport programs and the practices of sport leaders.

Ellis (1973) believes that humans are most human when engaged in play, since they are responding to intrinsic motives, are spontaneous, and are freely expressing their uniqueness. Current sport programs, as a highly specialized form of play, would appear to constrain playful athletes and restrict their freedom. Rather, when involved in traditionally structured sport, humans must, of necessity, suppress their humanity, their authenticity, their spontaneity, and their idiosyncratic nature. In most cases, failure to do so results in curtailment of playing time, if not banishment from the team.

The mass media has done an excellent job of promoting and providing high visibility for the professional coaching model. Concomitant with this phenomenon is the overexposure of victorious athletes and teams, the overemphasis on competition and winning, and the stress placed on visible, physical, objective, product outcomes. Overlooked or relegated to a distant second in terms of attention are outcomes related to the cognitive and affective areas of the encounter with sport (e.g. enjoyment, development of responsibility, moral integrity, and improved social relations). Rarely reaching the level of news or receiving minimal media exposure is the individual coach or program employing truly humanistic methods.

Since humanistic coaching behavior is quickly discounted by most athletic leaders, most coaches have not bothered to carefully analyze this model and consider how it could be applied in the sport setting. By refusing to objectively consider the implications of the humanistic model of sport, the coach's belief in the professional model is not only reaffirmed but also not threatened.

This circular reasoning in support of the prevailing belief system, bolstered by the media exposure of the professional model of sport, is not unique to sport or coaches, but is has resulted in, at best, a perfunctory consideration of humane systems of sport.

Another factor contributing to the current pervasive support for traditionally organized sport programs relates to the expectations of the athletic organization, the community, the coaching profession, the athletes, and the parents of the participants. Faw (cited in Rogers, 1969, p. 40) refers to these expectations as "institutional press." These forces are imposed on coaches and athletes alike and are somewhat beyond the control of either. The traditional coaching model is one characterized by manipulation, coercion, and a depersonalized system of human relationships, with the coach firmly established in a position of authority. This model constitutes a "press" on every coach. Breaking with the traditional model of coaching in order to realize humanistic goals is extremely difficult and would require going against the prevailing normative order (Danziger, 1980). This factor often prevents a coach from deviating from conventional coaching practice or leads to the early abandonment of initial attempts at humanizing the sport program.

Hellison's analysis suggests several reasons why coaches reject humanistic methods (1973). The first factor centers on the fact that the coach reflects society's emphasis on product values rather than humanistic or process concerns. A second factor relates to the coach's professional image, which is intertwined with the values of competition and achievement. Danziger (1980) supports this view and suggests that tradition and societal values are major forces which suppress the initiation and implementation of humanistic athletic programs. Yet, another factor which precludes employment of humanistic coaching methods identified by Hellison (1973) is the authoritarian orientation held by most coaches. This latter view is supported also by the work of Sage (1975) and Gensemer (1980).

Ulrich and Walker (1982) suggest that the lack of humanistic models of sport can be traced to two major factors. The first relates to society's narrow and yet widely accepted definition of the athletic coach, who is obliged by both the task and the nature of sport to act in certain ways. Society has limited the coach's role to the selection, organization, and deployment of talent in an efficient, time saving manner in order to win. The general public—the primary source of evaluation for the coach, the athlete, and the team—requires success (i.e. victory) in highly visible displays of prowess. Additionally, the athletes themselves exert great pressure on the coach, since they expect the coach to improve and refine their motor skills by intensive practice sessions and employment of the coach's expertise, and would rather not participate in "laborious and esoteric self-discovery techniques" (p. 72).

As a second factor, Ulrich and Walker (1982) point to the confused and often bewildering pattern resulting from the poorly defined relationship between, and limits of, the physical education and coaching professions, as a major obstacle in the formation of humanistic sport programs.

Within the sport world, the external pressures on "playing" have so increased that the athlete no longer has the luxury of truly playing, learning via mistakes and taking pre-mediatated, calculated risks, in order to enhance his/her individual learning and growth. Consequently, two significant situations arise, that is, certain individuals refuse to partake of such activities, while others literally "play the game" of playing the game at such a great loss to individual growth. Insistence by the adult leaders in sport that the athletes devote their entire being to the task of winning, sacrificing all other reasons for participation (i.e. intrinsic motives), has transformed what was initially the individual's play to work. When a player's only concern is the final outcome (or other externally imposed objectives), the athlete loses the opportunity for many pertinent, personal, and novel insights and discoveries inherent in the process (Gensemer, 1980).

Another factor which mitigates against humanistic sport programs relates to the place of sport in society. Authorities have repeatedly emphasized that sport mirrors society (Martens, 1978; Coakley, 1982; Eitzen & Sage, 1982). It comes as no surprise then that adult-sponsored sport is dominated by leadership which clearly reflects a belief in realistic behavioral principles. In a society which has so enthusiastically embraced behaviorism for most of the past century, to observe otherwise would be highly unexpected. However, it is from the assumptions derived from behaviorism that sport must extricate itself if it is to truly contribute in a positive manner to the development of young people. Alternative coaching behavior is required to move beyond behaviorally dominated sport activities if the goals of increased participation, sustained interest, enhanced mental health, and an active life-style are to be achieved.

Human movement, the ultimate end of which is the growth and development of the human body, represents the form of education most able to address growth along several dimensions: psychomotor, cognitive, and affective. Gensemer (1980) states: "It is important to note in this regard that any growth-directed effort, to the extent to which it takes seriously the individual, along with his consciousness and his freedom, is in the broad sense humanistic" (p. 142).

The sport experience, as a unique form of human movement, is truly a humanistic activity, despite efforts by some to the contrary. Sport seriously engages the individual, the individual's consciousness, and his/her freedom, in an endeavor which must be categorized as growth-promoting. However, as long as sport is conducted without regard for the individual's uniqueness, subjectivity, wholeness, and innate potential and instead gives priority to more objective outcomes and to the products rather than the process of the experience, the worthy ends identified previously as goals of the sport experience will never truly be attained. Unfortunately, sport is so absorbed with competition and winning that it rarely focuses on the participant's personal experience. Too much time is spent on the pursuit of victory and too little devoted to the athlete.

Why such a void in humanistic athletic leadership? Can it be that those dealing with human movement, on a regular basis, view the task of the athlete as a "closed" venture rather than an "open" one? Viewed in this manner, are their coaching practices then reduced to having the athlete perfect a singular response for each of a set of specific circumstances, to be performed at the command of the coach? Why is coaching so steeped in reductionistic, behavioral methodology, preferring as it apparently does to elicit certain, practiced, prepared responses to situations; in short, to perform as told rather than encourage the preparation of free-thinking, interpretative, analytical athletes who are capable of self-direction and independent motor decisions?

Sport must be administered in an open, democratic, and humanistic manner in which the individual is provided opportunities to achieve his/her potential. The sport establishment, however, is looked upon as being devoid (bereft) of creative educational plans and administrative structures which emphasize individuality, the participant, cooperation, etc. In other words, objectives other than winning and competition are a distant second in priority. Typically, the goals stressed are group performance, team unity, self-sacrifice for the good of the group, winning, and competition. The leadership in sport has been characterized as staunch conformists who wish to preserve elements of the status quo at almost any cost. Consequently, the dominant and pervasive elements of athletic programs are discipline and the keeping of order. Authoritative athletic leadership derived from the classic Western style of influencing others can be very gratifying to the coach issuing orders. It has certain advantages. It is quick and requires a minimum of knowledge about subordinates.

Moreover, since collaborative management or leadership techniques in athletics do not always satisfy ego needs of managers and coaches as thoroughly as do authoritative techniques, they are often overlooked in the egocentric sporting world.

Satisfaction from sports participation must be recognized for what it is (idiosyncratic), and the sport experience must be so because every person is different and unique. Yet, when one examines the data relative to coaching behavior, the patterns revealed indicate that coaches treat all athletes the same. Indeed, one of the most cited bits of coaching rhetoric, raised almost to the level of a basic principle of coaching, regarding the management of athletes includes statements like "be consistent," "treat all players the same," and "do not play favorites," etc.

It is suggested that the humanistic coaching model can provide the necessary framework for alternative coaching behavior. This humanistic model can overcome the weaknesses in the present system of athletics and at the same time enhance both the experience for the individual participant and facilitate improved motor performance. Likewise, humanistic sport will enhance the experience from the coach's vantage point, providing athletic leaders with opportunities to be real, to be genuine, to be authentic persons, and provide coaches with the opportunity to cease playing the role of "the coach."

PART II: HUMANISM AND SPORT

Sport has always been considered a vehicle for socialization. Participation in sport often is justified because of its supposed ability to develop the individual in preparation for successful integration into society. Indeed, it is easy to be overwhelmed by the extent to which the metaphor of sport as a proving ground and preparation for individuals planning to enter such diverse arenas of society as the military, politics, business, education, etc., is accepted and promoted. As such, and in spite of the disparagement offered by its detractors, sport is in a position to become a major factor in initiating change in society and contributing much to individual development.

However, there are those who assail the institution of sport as presently structured for its stagnancy and its resistance to change, its focus on discipline, and its efforts to maintain the existing order at the expense of all other outcomes. Questions continually arise as to the ability of sport to move beyond mere rhetoric and to truly contribute in a meaningful way to the development of people who must live in a world in which change occurs at a rapidly increasing pace. Challenges abound from every direction related to the ability of sport to alter its course to accomplish humanistic goals traditionally not included among its objectives. The question remains: Can the structure of sport, presently best characterized as a conservative and inflexible institution, be modified to truly promote and attend to the growth of the individual athlete?

The world needs individuals who are sensitive and can respond effectively when confronted with new problems and situations. Such adaptive people must be able to perceive and identify critical information embedded in novel and complex situations in order to make accurate mature judgments upon which to base his/her behavior.

Sport, humanistically administered, can contribute immensely to the development of such abilities by providing opportunities for making relevant decisions and analysis of the processes involved therein, as well as encouraging free expression, creativity, imagination, and thinking, all in a non-threatening, facilitative environment. Sport, as a type of play behavior, should have adaptive significance for the participant, in the sense that it enlarges the breadth of experience that the athlete has to draw upon in facing novel situations and variable conditions (Ellis, 1973).

Similarly, Gensemer (1980) reinforces this thought: "The execution of most motor skills is essentially a fluid endeavor. The accomplishment of any motor performance generally requires that the performer be either versatile, adaptable, or self-expressive. . . . In no case, however, is everything static. Situations are always changing" (p. 54).

Therefore, athletics should be process-oriented. Athletics may have the greatest potential for enhancing those qualities outlined above by Gensemer (i.e. "fluid intelligence") (Horn & Cattell, 1966). Human movement, including athletics, is a complete human activity, which requires the engagement of both the mental and physical faculties of the athlete.

Humanistic athletics places a premium on creativity and imagination rather than on rote, mechanistic responses, on planning and initiative instead of conformity and following directions, and on problem solving rather than on obedience. The fluid nature of most team sports provides opportunities for considerable variability in individual performance. And indeed this is the case, for athletic performance in such open, variable environments is highly stylized, idiosyncratic, and personalized, despite the desperate attempts of coaches at homogenization of motor performance (Gensemer, 1980). Athletic competition set within open and unstable environments precludes predictable, mechanistic motor behavior. Instead, motor behavior in sport must be characterized by behavioral flexibility rather than stability in order to achieve success.

Gensemer (1980), discussing this aspect of motor performance, continues:

> It is entirely logical, then, to conclude that a humanistic attitude . . . is the reasonable way to arrange these experiences. Open skills require adaptability, and humanism facilitates it. Thus the movement freedom of the humanistic approach is an asset, for there is no need for all . . . to arrive at the same end of mechanical performance. Rather, there can be an acceptance of any technique which accomplishes the objective. (p. 117)

Sport and athletic competition involves direct motor experiences. All human motor behavior generates kinesthetic sensations about his/her body relative to such movement which is received and perceived by the mover. This motoric source of information about oneself (i.e. kinesthetic data) always leads to increased knowledge about one's inner self. The enhancement of the ability to know oneself is truly a major goal of humanism. From the preceding, it can be concluded that sport, as a highly specialized form of human movement, must be interpreted as a humanistic experience. To do otherwise is to deny a situation which is irrefutable. The participant learns much through the motor experience, especially in the sport setting, which must be categorized as personal, subjective, kinesthetic, etc., all of which contributes to individual, idiopathic growth and development.

Therefore, it follows that the very essence of the sport experience for the performer will be in the actual process of participation. The process becomes the central focus of the experience, much more important than what is achieved (i.e. product) and tantamount to all other externally introduced goals.

The valued outcomes of the athletic experience are matters which are meaningful to athletes in a personal, subjective, and idiosyncratic way. Humanistic sport is based on the concept that the only meaningful learnings are self-discovered.

Traditionally structured sport programs consider winning its major goal. It has been concerned almost exclusively with the "what" and the "how much." It has emphasized products and the quantitative factors of athletic accomplishments. Humanistic sport experiences focus more on how athletes perform rather than what they achieve; the process of playing is more critical than the results of the activity or the activity itself.

Process-centered athletics aims at the development of the inner person, which allows athletes to be authors of their own experiences.

A humanistic conception of sport generally views the experience of playing as a source of pleasure, rather than an instrument for competition or as a vehicle to status, prestige, etc. In other words, humanistically organized sport attempts to eliminate the distinction between means and ends, instead conceptualizing playing as the goal of the activity and thereby stressing the importance of the here-and-now experience of the participant. In this way sport can magnify, in a qualitative sense, its contribution to the athletes and their development.

Humanistic sport programs are those in which the environment encourages successful personal encounter; where ideas, facts, and feelings are openly expressed; where conflict is not hidden; where emotions share equal importance with motor skill development and demonstration; and where activities are a combination of athlete interests and the goals of the program.

Humanistic athletics has at its very foundation the belief that the inner feelings, emotions, and sensations resulting from sport experiences leading to self-discovery will be manifested in enhanced positive attitudes of self.

Envision for a moment the truly astounding, powerful effect that the sport encounter can have on athletes. If the aforementioned humanistic objectives can be incorporated into adult-sponsored athletic programs, added as such to the traditionally promoted outcomes of enhanced motor proficiency, knowledge of the game, etc., at that point in time sport will have become all it can be. Sport, structured and organized humanistically, can be a multidimensional vehicle for the total development of the participants.

PART III: HUMANISM AND THE COACH

What is to be gained by the athletic coach if sport is restructured based on humanistic tenets? Why should a coach support a shift to humanism and humanistic sport programs? These and other questions are raised by both proponents and opponents of humanized sport. Coaches need to know "what's in it for them," and parents must have their questions resolved adequately and in a confident manner. More importantly, however, are the responses provided to the athletes, as they wish to understand not only the nature of such significant changes (many which challenge their basic assumptions about sport and their beliefs about how athletic programs should be conducted) but also to gain an under- standing of the long-term benefits of such modifications.

At the very foundation of humanism is its belief in the individual's autonomy and freedom. A logical extension of this tenet is that athletic programs guided by humanistic concepts enable and encourage all par- ticipants, including adult leaders, to be genuine and authentic. The coach will no longer have to "play" the role of the coach or don a "coach- ing face" when confronted with athletes. He/she can be him/herself and in effect present his/her real self to the athletes. A shift to humanism would allow the coach the opportunity to be free to be him/herself. Hu- manistic tenets incorporated into sport programs would result in hu- manistic coaches who can retain their own identity and authenticity while simultaneously allowing and encouraging the athletes to develop their personal identities, their own values, and to develop in their own idiosyncratic way.

No longer must the coach be the sole source of direction, knowledge, and wisdom. The shift to humanism will be viewed by many adult leaders in sport as a positive modification, especially those long dissatis- fied with the pressures usually associated with the assumption of control of athletic teams.

Humanistically designed sport requires that the conventional coach- ing role be changed from information-giver and director to facilitator and equal partner in the venture of sport. The sport encounter will be- come a jointly planned endeavor when sport programs are humanized. Long gone will be the days when all eyes focused on the coach for answers and directions. Rather, the coach, the individual athlete, and the team will search for the possible responses for each of the many situ- ations and conditions which are an inevitable, intrinsic, and characteris- tic part of sport. Together, these problems will be resolved.

Another major outcome of a shift to humanism in sport will be the implementation of humanistic evaluation of the coach's performance. Since the coach will have become a facilitator of the athletes' total growth and development in many areas, the coach's win-loss record will be only one of many factors considered in the evaluation process. Measures of coaching effectiveness will have to be redefined, broadened in scope, and become more all-inclusive. Indeed, items such as the motor profi- ciency of individual athletes, cognitive abilities as reflected in analysis of motor skills as well as in strategic decision making, and knowledge of training regimes would be acceptable sources of data relative to judging in several areas (e.g. mental, moral, psychomotor, physiological). These outcomes can be employed to measure the effectiveness of the coach, thereby minimizing the reliance upon the team's win-loss record.

A brief description of current coaching behavior might elucidate the major differences between conventional leadership and humanistically structured sport programs. At the present time, the typical athletic coach makes all relevant decisions related to the contest with one significant exception. Regardless of how domineering, autocratic, or directive a coach may be, the performer always has the ball in his/her court, so to speak. At the point of execution the athlete is free, and rightly so, to move and do as he/she wishes. Usually, the athlete's movements are based upon his/her perception and interpretation of the immediate environmental conditions, buttressed by the long hours of practice and study under the tutelage of the coach. While the influence of the coach on the performer cannot be denied, at the moment of impact the athlete is in total command of his/her actions and decides what to do, how to do it, etc. This brief vignette, repeated continually throughout the competitive contest, is what makes sport so unpredictable and accounts, in part, for its great attraction. The play is literally out of the hands of the coach, despite the fact that often the independent athlete must answer to the coach for such independence, especially if the unpredictable or risk-taking action failed to achieve its intent.

Any description of current conventional coaching behavior must be characterized by the coach setting line ups, making substitutions, calling time-outs, calling offensive and defensive plays, etc. In effect, the coach does everything but the most important thing, that is, play. The athletes, it seems, play on the coach's team and have the privilege to perform in the adult-led game. A direct outcome of such control resting in the hands of the coach is the creation, nurturance, and, indeed, the anticipation of dependent athletes in a sort of symbiotic relationship in which athletes are led to believe in their coach and his/her infallible system. What is effected, then, is a system whereby the non-player (i.e. the coach) becomes responsible for and a critical factor in the actions of the players. The athletes, in turn, often reject, resist, and outwardly balk at efforts to give them decision-making opportunities, thereby reinforcing the coach's belief that he/she is not only in control but also is indispensable to the functioning of the team. The athletes have become accustomed to this system, especially the professional model of coaching behavior as delineated previously and, indeed, often are its most vociferous proponents. Moreover, the humanistic coach at this point in time is met with scorn, distrust, and disapproval and appears to be a failure and weak as a leader and a coach, as well as someone odd and totally out of step with the times. The adults have gained control of the athletes' game and the athletes, for the most part, have accepted this notion whole-heartedly and would have it no other way!

The reader should note that the above description of the current state of affairs creates much pressure on both the athlete and the coach. The present condition of sport, embued with the tenets of the professional model of coaching, places both the coach and athletes in very narrowly defined and confining roles. At the present time, the athlete or coach who behaves otherwise runs the risk of being identified as being odd or, worse yet, being banned from participation altogether.

The typical coach interprets the main task of athletic leadership as that of harnessing the energy of athletes so that the goals of improved motor performance and victory will be achieved. This coach sees him/herself as responsible for organizing the team's activities, and therefore, he/she must motivate and direct the athletes, control their actions, and modify the behavior of those members of the team in such ways that the goals of the group will be achieved. Implied in these actions is the view that athletes would be, if left unsupervised, apathetic to, or resistant to, the goals of the team. Consequently, athletes must be rewarded, punished, and prodded so that they strive to improve and to win — goals identified by the adult leader as the most important products of the experience. The implications of such a profile of coaching behavior are clear: (1) athletes prefer to be guided or led; (2) athletes are incapable of self-directed activity; and (3) behavior controls are required to keep athletes on-task.

Humanism constitutes a realistic alternative to such a state of affairs and provides a relevant, useful alternative to coaches who are dissatisfied with conventional coaching leadership. Decisions will be made by both athletes and coaches acting and thinking together. The humanistic coach organizes resources, materials, and activities in such a way that all persons involved can work together toward identifying and achieving their own goals. Inherent in this view is that intrinsic motivation for behavior resides in each participant. The coach, then, goes about creating opportunities where athletes can freely use their innate potential, encouraging growth and change, and creating an atmosphere in which each performer believes that his/her ability and potential is valued and where his/her capacity for responsible behavior and creativity is trusted and prized (Rogers, 1969). In direct contrast with the professional model of athletic leadership, a function of the humanistic coach is to become increasingly dispensable and to enable athletes to rely upon the coach less and less and upon him/herself more and more. In this type of structure, responsibility, authority, and initiative is diffused throughout the team. This concept insures the best possible use of available knowledges, skills, and competencies, thereby enhancing the process of decision making as well as maximizing the development of all involved in the athletic endeavor.

Another positive aspect of moving sport in a humanistic direction relates to the coach's role as the distributor of rewards and sanctions. A major focus of humanistic thought relates to the development of an internal source of evaluation. Self-analysis and self-evaluation, as techniques capable of leading the individual to a better understanding of self, a major precept of humanism, would relieve coaches of a difficult, time-consuming, and often distasteful task.

In a humanistic program coaches would assist athletes in their attempts to become aware of their capabilities and limitations, would facilitate their efforts to set meaningful, realistic, and personal goals, and would provide feedback about the athlete's efforts. Sport structured humanistically encourages, almost demands, that the athlete continually assess him/herself and, therefore, encourages the athlete to become cognizant of the fact that the individual is the best source of such dispensations. Humanistic sport encourages and facilitates the process by which individuals come to rely on their own faculties as sources of feedback relative to personal, subjective growth and development.

PART IV: HUMANISM AND THE ATHLETE

What are the benefits to be accrued by athletes if sport programs and coaching behavior is modified so that it emphasizes humanistic precepts? How will participants' encounter with sport be different?

Humanistic coaching, within an athlete-centered sport program, will promote self-fulfillment. Specifically, the athletes should realize their own positive human potential, become well-acquainted with the self, and reach full functioning, not only in sport, but in all aspects of life. In short, humanistic sport will foster the accomplishment of those goals commonly believed (and widely accepted) and attributed to the phenomenon of sport as delineated previously in Chapter 1.

Athlete-centered coaching behavior and the resulting humanization of the entire sport scene should lead to the development of athletes more self-directed, and far less dependent, to a significantly greater extent than at present. Since these athletes would be encouraged and expected to be more autonomous and more reliant on inner determinants, dependence upon adults in the sport situation will be drastically reduced. Moreover, since the participants will be guided by personal and, therefore, meaningful inner motives, they will become less anxious for extrinsic rewards, prestige, and recognition. In effect, athletes will be free to pursue their goals, released from the often confining, intimidating, and inhibiting externally induced need to seek the coach's approval.

Sage (1972) suggests that current coaching practice, influenced as it is by various situational conditions, including overemphasis on winning and other objective, impersonal standards, requires that coaches make "cool cognitive analysis of the needs of the team" and "disregard the individual needs of the players" (p. 58). Sage continues and describes the need for coaches to distance themselves from athletes:

> In general, the coach cannot become too affectively involved with those whom he is coaching, he must detach and depersonalize his relationships with the players in order to make effective decisions with regard to player selection, devising strategies, and a host of other decisions which require taking a hard line for the benefit of the team. (p. 58)

The implication is that to be effective, a coach cannot allow him/herself to become affectively involved with individuals on the team. The coach must establish and maintain his/her distance from the players.

The coach who centers the sport experience on the participant will be able to perceive and accept each athlete in his/her own right and can achieve this without the urge to classify, to compare, or to categorize the individual. Released from the pressure of winning, the coach is free to relate to athletes on a more personal level, thereby building strong affective ties to individuals on his/her team. Athletes, in such a situation, will feel they are being observed and valued for themselves, with the coach making decisions relative to the innate potential of each participant, in view of each individual's needs and motives, rather than feeling that they are being judged by some remote and unreasonable standard or average (or at least standards with which the athlete has little input). The individual athlete will gain, not only a better understanding of his/her capabilities, but also a deeper acceptance of him/herself.

When coaches allow for freedom of expression, athletes become more at liberty to be true to themselves, to pursue their own interests, and to determine their own values. Gensemer (1980) believes that: "When coaches minimize rules, encourage discovery and self-appropriated learning, then athletics can foster the kinds of freedom that result in more meaningful knowledge — generally referred to as conceptual learning" (p. 39).

Such self-discovery involves analysis, logic, and synthesis in a self-governing operation. The result would be not only self-discovery and knowledge of self but also a sharpening of the learning capacity itself. Athletes acquire an ability to make future discoveries once these skills are developed. Gensemer (1980) adds that "an atmosphere of psychological freedom appears to assist athletes in becoming organized, consistent, and self-controlled humans" (p. 39).

Sport, as a form of play, can and should also facilitate behavioral variability of the athlete and heighten the development of future adaptation to unpredictable circumstances (Ellis, 1973). Since sport confronts the athlete with predominantly varying, unstable, and changing conditions and environments, an encounter with sport which encourages the participants to not only freely perceive these aspects but also to respond in an open, unrestrained fashion facilitates growth of a critical nature. Ellis (1973) believes that this growth is not limited to the sport setting but has wider application which extends into all facets of the individual's life.

> Individuals that have generated relatively large numbers of novel responses over and above those required for immediate existence will acquire information as a by-product that will tend to convey an advantage when circumstances change. In other words, . . . the greater chance it will have of surviving change in its habitate. (p. 114)

It is clear that when athletes are given meaningful control of their sporting activities the "dropping-out" phenomenon can be addressed in a unique manner and quite possibly resolved to the satisfaction of all concerned. Rogers' (1969) argument in favor of the creation of humanistic academic environments extended to include sport, leads to the proposition that when athletes perceive that they are free to follow their own goals, most of them will invest more of themselves in their efforts, work harder, and retain more of what they have experienced, than in conventional sport dominated by the professional coaching model. If athletes have identified meaningful personal goals, and if they are free to choose and develop activities which lead to achievement of these goals, it is impossible for the athlete not to enjoy, not to get excited about the sport experience. A recent study by Fisher et al. (1982) focused on coach-athlete interaction and team atmosphere. Fisher et al. concluded that: "There is more satisfaction to be derived when one is an active participant in the learning process . . . and more member satisfaction with team climates that foster involvement" (p. 398).

In a humanized program, the athletes' interest in the activity will be greatly increased. This should result in fewer dropouts as well as maintenance of higher participation levels over a longer period of time. It may even result in a significant increase in the number of adults who come to value sport and human movement as a result of their positive competitive sport experience so highly as to make it a significant part of their everyday living. In effect, humanistic athletic experiences could affect the general health and well-being of an individual for his/her lifetime.

To reiterate and to directly address the questions posed at the start of this chapter, it should be clear that humanistic sport programs and humanistic athletic leadership will affect athletes in the following ways:

The athlete:

- will feel free to express his/her feelings (positive and negative) toward athletes, coaches, and the sport experience.
- will discover he/she has a responsibility for his/her own development as he/she becomes more directly involved in the sport.
- will feel free and confident to go in his/her own direction in pursuit of full development, buoyed with the knowledge that the coach will understand and encourage such a pursuit.
- will find that both the awe and anxiety often associated with the experience of adult leadership and his/her resistance to authority diminish as she/he discovers the humaneness, the imperfectness, the acceptance, the empathy, and the fallibility of the coach.
- will find that sport enables him/her to directly and subjectively confront the problem of meaning in life.

Chapter 4

THEORY INTO PRACTICE: EXAMPLES OF HUMANISTIC COACHING BEHAVIOR

PART I: BECOMING A HUMANISTIC COACH

THE PURPOSE of this section is to suggest guidelines as well as specific measures that will facilitate the move to humanized sport. Specifically, the ideas presented here should assist individual coaches and athletic organizations in their efforts to incorporate humanistic principles into sport and athletic coaching and, when instituted, will facilitate changes in the pervasive professional-coaching behavior.

1. A major characteristic of modern life is change, which, like death and taxes, has become accepted as an inevitable part of daily living. Modern man devotes much of his/her early years preparing to deal with the near revolutionary pace of change. The turbulence and stress often associated with the phenomenon of change often accounts for the common reactions to initiatives for change: apathy, indifference, defensiveness, resistance, anxiety, and fear.

The process of change is usually difficult and can quickly become a highly charged experience, since it requires attitudinal, behavioral, and factual reorganization (Cheffers & Evaul, 1978). Such modifications can be threatening to the individual. "Any suggestion for change implies that something can be done better. The immediate reaction is one of mistrust; the power structure would like to believe that what exists is satisfactory!" (Heitman & Kneer, p. 285).

Changes as those proposed here are guaranteed to generate controversy. It takes courage and a firm belief in one's convictions to attempt a novel approach, and many adult sport leaders, understandably, are not capable of, nor well-suited for, such actions. Coaches and adult sponsors of sport, in many cases volunteers filling a need for supervision, are often ill-prepared. Many times, the coach is a parent, who possesses little knowledge of the specifics of the activity. Also, many innovations are not implemented or fail when they are because the individuals involved are not properly prepared to support such changes. Change is difficult, hard work, and often threatening. As a result of these two latter factors coaches and leaders feel insecure, which renders them basically resentful and resistant to imposed change and ineffectual as initiators of meaningful change.

A major deterrent to the institution of justifiable change has been the inflexibility of coaches. Many innovative programs have been doomed to failure because of such resistance to change. A component of this resistance can be accounted for by the fact that coaches enter athletics and sport prepared for and fully endorsing a coach-centered approach.

Even coaches considered professionally prepared are often not predisposed to favor, support, or initiate change, especially those changes basic to the humanization of sport. Gensemer (1980), after a review of data pertaining to the psychological profile of physical education teachers, the professional field in which a large majority of athletic coaches receive their preparation, believes that they "probably feel uncomfortable in settings that allow the freedoms which are the foundation of humanistic teaching" (p. 45).

The implication of such data is that it is quite possible that those entering the field of coaching and athletic leadership possess characteristics which mitigates against their initiating change or supporting open, interactive, and facilitative systems of sport. Albaugh (1972), after examination of athletic coaches' attitudes toward learning, supports this view. Sage (1975) also found support for this notion based on his extensive work which examined the socialization of coaches.

The widely accepted structure of sport affords a refuge to some, and to deliberately "rock the boat" can be terribly unnerving. As stated previously, the pressures to conform are indeed strong within and without the coaching profession, resulting in and accounting for both professional homogenization and the prevailing coaching stereotypes. Conditions prerequisite to implementation of humanistic coaching practice are rarely observed, because they mean a real departure in our approach to sport.

Changes brought on by external forces or via non-humanistic methods are typically ephemeral in effect, perfunctory in nature, or meaningless. Cheffers and Evaul (1978) believe that: "Externally applied pressures will bring about change but the results cannot be guaranteed, nor can they be fully predicted" (p. 211).

Intrinsically motivated change tends to be more permanent and more enduring. Moriarty et al. (1977) have field-tested a model for change agent research which holds much promise for effecting change. The focus of this model is on stimulating change based on the individual's or program's recognition of the need for change, employing a humanistic model for change. Specifically, the agency to be changed takes an active role in initiating, planning for, and evaluating the needed changes.

A coach must be secure in his/her own self-concept to undertake such a program of change. In order to relinquish the accepted time-honored role of the coach as the supreme leader, one must understand and accept oneself first. Coaches and other adult leaders must have a healthy acceptance of self, and their need to feel competent must be met so that attention can be turned away from themselves and toward the athletes.

In other words, coaches must feel good about their being and accomplishments so as to not use their athletes to satisfy their needs for self-actualization or self-aggrandizement. Rather, coaches must focus on the sport experience as a vehicle to satisfy the needs of the athletes, as well as an activity with the potential to strengthen the athletes' feelings of self-worth.

Once it is forgotten that the sport participant (i.e. player) is at the center of his/her own universe, with a personal history, subjectivity, and intentionality all his/her own, the coach starts treating the athlete like a "thing," an object. This person-to-be-done-to (i.e. object) will help the coach (and be used to) confirm his/her status as a leader of athletes.

2. The amount of freedom, inherent in the process of humanizing sport, which can be given a group is not particularly important. What is important is that the freedom provided is real, is not spitefully or hesitantly given by the adult supervisor, and is perceived as authentic by the athletes (Rogers, 1969). Rejeski et al. (1979), addressing youth sport programs in particular, state aptly: "Ultimately, it is the perceptions of children, not adult intentions, which determine the consequence of particular coaching behaviors (p. 317).

It is important to reiterate Rogers' point related to the institution of change characterized by humanistic tenets. Rogers (1969) believed that it is more important to give freedom freely, honestly, and securely; that is, with an attitude which is congruent with the actions of the leader. How much freedom a leader provides is secondary at that particular moment. The leader's actions are much more powerful in their effect. Certainly, this argument can and should be extended to all levels of sport.

The attitude of the coach is critical when implementing changes as radical as those proposed here. The transition to humanistic sport will be facilitated if the coach can radiate behavior which first indicates that the coach's concept of the athlete is tentative and open to revision, and second, conveys the view that he/she does not and cannot ever fully know the athlete's full potential. In this way, the coach invites the participant to explore the limits of his/her awareness and encourages risk-taking by the athletes as they pursue self-awareness. Such coaching behavior also encourages the athlete to go beyond concepts previously held by the coach of the athlete, to innovate, to diverge, and to reveal new aspects of their being, to be him/herself, and to be authentic. The coach does this rather than shut off, stifle, or constrain the athletes as they endeavor to know themselves and to become genuine individuals.

A critical aspect of a humanized sport setting is the ability of the coach to convey the expectation that the athlete is trustworthy, responsible, capable of self-direction, and able to identify relevant goals. Jourard (1968) claims that: "The teacher who turns on the dull pupil, the coach who elicits a magnificent performance from someone of whom it could not have been expected, are people who *themselves* have an image of the *pupil's possibilities;* and they are effective in realizing their images" (p. 126).

3. The goals one is striving to achieve must be clearly understood, kept in sight at all times, and constantly in the forefront. Athletes conditioned to accept the coach-centered approach, which strictly regiments their behavior, usually have not experienced or learned to think independently. If measures are not incorporated into the implementation process, athletes may feel confused and lost (Heitman & Kneer, 1976).

A major task of the coach seriously considering a change is to clearly identify the goals of the athletic program related to the incorporation of humanistic principles. These goal-statements should not only be clearly enunciated but also explained to the athletes involved. From the first day of anticipated change the athletes should be aware of such modifications. Opportunities for discussion for the purpose of clarification, questioning, etc., must be furnished to the athlete.

Once freedom is given, some athletes may feel that they are at liberty to do as they please. Often, this will occur at the expense of other athletes, the team as a whole, and learning in general. Athletes, at each stage of implementation, need to understand clearly what is expected of them and how they can proceed in the sport-learning process (Heitman & Kneer, 1976).

A second consideration here is that the leader must not lose sight of these changes. Shifting to humanism requires that the coach remember that the individual is of utmost importance, and related changes must be kept in the forefront of the athletic endeavor if humanism is to have its planned effect. To do otherwise will result in confusion and chaos for the participants and greatly restrict the planned broad effect of humanism to sport.

4. It is strongly suggested that a gradual weaning process, moving from the traditional spoon-feeding approach to a totally self-directed program, be employed. This process, consisting of a program of small, incremental steps whereby the coach can introduce athletes to increasing degrees of uncertainty, to progressively more challenging problem circumstances, and to increasing degrees of frustration, will enhance the athlete's potential for problem resolution and autonomy. The athletic leadership should move slowly at first, experimenting with "opening" the sport experience and testing the waters as change is initiated.

The leadership should relinquish control gradually (and with the comfort of both coaches and performers in mind) until that degree of freedom and openness is attained which administrators, coaches, and participants can manage. It is just as difficult for athletes to adjust to newly gained freedom thrust quickly and all at once as it will be for traditional authoritarian coaches to change their leadership style. However, at some point the athletes must struggle on their own when they arrive at impasses and obstacles.

5. An important precursor to the athlete's transition from a conforming, obedient, pawn of the coach to a truly self-directed, self-reliant, independent player is the creation by the coach of an environment in which the athlete must confront meaningful and relevant problems. Only when confronted with problematical circumstances which test and fully challenge him/her does the athlete discover and extend his/her true potential. Jourard (1968) states it aptly: "Man grows and fulfills his peculiar possibilities — physical, mental, and spiritual — *only through struggle,* and, moreover, struggle to find his own way" (p. 131). The presentation of obstacles in the form of relevant challenges is vital to the athlete's pursuit of self-discovery.

These problems probably should emerge from interaction between coach and player, player and environment, and player and player or team. Faced with such sport-related problems and provided with the authority to plan and act upon them, the athlete's ability to choose from among logical alternatives and make appropriate decisions will be enhanced. In addition, coaches should support and challenge athletes so that they acquire a greater ease and awareness of themselves and can release the spontaneous and real behaviors so characteristic of an authentic personality.

Assuming that there is an educational intent to the athlete's encounter with sport, the player must learn by doing, by trying, by acting. The coach's role is very clear. It is the responsibility of the coach to create and present complex, difficult challenges and problems in order to provide the athlete with opportunities to discover how well he/she can perform, as well as explore the limits of his/her awareness and capacities. The coach can and, at times, must provide assistance in varied forms, but it is the athlete who should evaluate the consequences of his/her judgment and choices, analyze his/her motor behavior, and make decisions regarding personal goals and standards.

6. Implicit in humanistic coaching is the concept of psychological flexibility. Variable leadership styles which offer athletes opportunities for their own decision making, as contrasted with traditional coaching behavior, should characterize the atmosphere on competitive playing fields. The coach who demonstrates flexibility can adjust and adapt his/her behavior, leadership style, etc., to the needs, characteristics, and abilities of the athlete. It is not suggested, then, that all coaches should act in an identical manner to all athletes in the particular sport setting. Rather, the coach needs to behave with sensitivity and to respond to athletes individually.

For most participants, the openness, freedom, and opportunity for self-directed learning and self-discovery will be welcomed. For some, however, given their unique stage of development, their personality structure, and/or expectations related to sport, this approach will not initially be appealing. Athletes themselves, the greatest benefactors of humanism in sport, may not be receptive to the sudden responsibility for self-direction given by a well-intentioned coach. Certainly, some athletes will feel threatened by this approach, repulsed by what they perceive to be a major flaw or defect in their leader, or simply bewildered by the number of decisions inherent in such a change. Still others will feel cheated and feel their efforts will be for naught, since their coach will be viewed as weak and too soft to nurture their progress as an athlete.

In the humanistic model, however, the coach can devote more time to such individuals, for he/she will have discarded the traditional approach to coaching; that is, maintaining a consistent, unchanging pattern of behavior, all with the intent of treating all athletes equally and identically. The coach, then, numbers among his/her objectives the accommodation of those athletes who do not wish or desire freedom, those not yet ready to deal effectively with such openness (e.g. individuals who are threatened, anxious, etc., at the thought of taking responsibility for their behavior) and for those who prefer, at their particular stage of maturity, to be instructed and guided in a more traditional fashion. This latter group, while they may be "spoon-fed" for some time, nevertheless, will be guided and assisted to eventually take charge of themselves and their encounter with sport. A humanistic approach to athletic coaching supports and encourages individualized strategies which make the above methods feasible and practical.

The success of humanized sport depends upon coaches who try to be genuine, honest, open, true to themselves, in essence to be more human. It is unfortunate that so many coaches strive to be perfect coaches in the professional mold, to be the eternal source of wisdom on the field, and to achieve the status of mythical hero-gods.

Coaches such as these, who believe they possess the power and the expertise required to identify the athlete's potential and willingly accept responsibility for the athlete's accomplishments, put themselves in an untenable and vulnerable position, which is also often barren of interaction, involvement, and communication of any significant consequence.

The humanistic changes discussed here will not only broaden the experience for the performer but in turn will liberate the coach from the current constrained and narrowly defined role in sport and society.

PART II: HUMANISTIC PRINCIPLES
APPLIED TO ATHLETIC COACHING

What are the specific implications of applying the principles of humanism to athletic coaching? What behaviors are prescribed for leaders of sport and especially athletic coaches by a humanistic agenda? How should the coach behave within the context of an athletic program committed to humanism?

The essence of humanistic athletic leadership behavior is summarized in Table 1.

Table 1

THE PRINCIPLES OF HUMANISTIC PSYCHOLOGY
APPLIED TO ATHLETIC COACHING

Principle	Application
Success promotion	Athletes' goals count, too
Positive Regard	Coaches value athletes
Involvement	Athletes get excited
Interaction	Athletes are heard
Cognitive processes	Athletes think
Congruence	Coaches are authentic
Empathy	Athletes' feelings count

An examination of each of these seven principles will facilitate the generation of specific recommendations for coaching behavior and thereby enhance the explication and application of humanism to sport.

SUCCESS PROMOTION

A major component of humanistic thought focuses on the individual's role in goal setting. The identification and establishment of personal and subjective goals by the athlete is critical to athletic programs desirous of incorporating humanism into their organization. By fostering and supporting a climate in which performers take responsibility for their behavior, guided by a process of self-determination, the organization insures success for athletes. By such actions, the leaders of the athletic program demonstrate faith and trust in the individual's personal and unique encounter with sport.

Coaches share and support the athletes' images of possibility and set about releasing and actualizing these (Jourard, 1968). Given a nurturing environment and the organization's support, the individual athlete who, more than anyone, is aware of his/her needs, ambitions, abilities, etc. (i.e. knows his/herself), will successfully identify realistic, yet personal goals. These goals, attainable, subjective, and meaningful, will set the tone of the athlete's endeavor with sport. The success of each athlete, as well as the team as a whole, would be heightened since the coach would no longer assume that his/her goals are attractive to the athletes. Research has shown again and again that the goals of the athletic leader too often conflict with those of the athletes. By refusing to hold the athlete to goals externally generated by coaches or the athletic organization, the leaders again express their belief that the performer is their central concern and, thereby, just about guarantees the athlete a successful sport experience.

A second component of success promotion relates to the evaluation of the progress of the athlete. Once the athlete has identified personal goals of the sport experience, the leadership encourages and fully anticipates the development of the performer's ability to analyze and evaluate his/her performance. Self-evaluation can never be anything but humanistic, although at times it can be biased, harsh, and hypercritical. While an athlete may be disappointed or discouraged about his/her performance, within a humanistic evaluation process he/she will not be compared to group performance or held to objective standards by significant others (i.e. the coach, parents, peers). In short, the process of preparing athletes to independently determine goals is, in effect, an inherently success-promoting technique. By insisting on an evaluation process which centers on the athlete's subjective experience while simultaneously rejecting the traditional reliance on group performance, goals, and standards, the leaders of sport insure that the athlete's subjective experience with sport will be preserved and become the basis for individual growth and development.

POSITIVE REGARD

Application of this principle requires that coaches value athletes as individuals. To do this, an athletic coach must treat performers, not only as infielders, goalies, quarterbacks, or milers, but as people valued for their uniqueness and humanness. The coach must prize, better yet celebrate, each individual for their unique human character. The application of this principle of humanism mandates that the coach never lose sight of the fact that beneath all the athletic equipment, dirt, sweat, bravado, and machismo, there is a warm, anxious, and lovable person, full of life and brimming with emotions, in need of acceptance, encouragement, and deserving of respect and dignity, that is, a high positive regard. These needs are common to all people, athletic or otherwise. The coach, then, should provide feedback, reinforcement, criticism, etc., of the athlete's behavior, separate and distinct from the individual's person, in order to continually encourage the athlete, to inspire the athlete to work and mature, and to keep foremost in the athlete-coach relationship the athlete's potential for goodness and growth. The coach, in order to provide the athlete with a high positive regard, must be able to take joy in or at least provide respect for and treat with dignity the person who is the athlete, in addition to working with the athlete-person.

Coaches should also provide support for the athletes as they confront the challenges inherent in a humanistic sport setting. Coaches who support athletes as they struggle with sport problems, decision making, etc., will foster the development of the athlete's self-awareness and will facilitate the emergence of spontaneous and genuine behaviors and, eventually, an authentic person.

INVOLVEMENT

Within a humanistic framework of sport, athletes get excited. The motivation in such programs is high. Performers realize that their destiny is self-determined to a point and are "turned on" by the prospect of being an equal partner in the sporting venture. Enthusiastic and exuberant behavior is commonplace, because the athlete can be real and genuine within a humanistic context, freed from the fear of losing face, freed from the distractions caused by efforts to play the role of an athlete (e.g. act like a professional athlete), and freed from anxiety about the coach's perception and assessment of his/her ability. The athlete in humanistic programs is free to be him/herself within the adventure that is sport.

There is excitement and happiness everywhere in humanistic programs, because the games, once again, belong to the players. External factors (e.g. spectators, expert coaches, the media) are placed a distant second to the needs, abilities, and decisions of the performers.

Another facet of the application of this principle to sport is the athlete's meaningful participation in the activity. Performers are motivated not only because they must make a multitude of important and relevant decisions about their performance, the contest, and the team but also because they observe that both their decisions and the personal process whereby decisions were arrived at are respected by the leader. The athlete soon learns that the activity revolves about his/her involvement.

Yet another reason for the often intense, animated participation in humanistic sport can be accounted for by the personal nature of such programs. The athlete establishes meaningful and personal goals and then designs activities to facilitate the attainment of such goals. If the athlete decides to pursue the sport (i.e. chooses not to drop out), then, in effect, he/she is participating in an athletic program structured on his/ her needs, desires, and personal goals. For these reasons, humanistic athletic programs should be characterized by high levels of motivation. Indeed, how could it be otherwise?

INTERACTION

Humanistic athletic organizations provide numerous opportunities to hear and truly listen to their athletes. Athletes are encouraged to speak out, to question, and to interact in important ways about relevant issues and concerns. Not only are interactive opportunities provided, but there is active support for the athlete. Moves are initiated to demonstrate to the athlete their equality in the ensuing interaction. Humanistic coaches encourage, and sometimes demand, player-coach and player-player interaction in order to achieve several goals related to the growth and development of the athlete.

Data reported by Carron and Bennett (1977) relate to the provision of meaningful interaction between players and coaches. They suggest that greater amounts of interaction and exchanging control behavior (i.e. both coaches and athletes exert and receive control) are significant factors in maintaining motivation of athletes as well as reducing the number of dropouts from sport.

An important characteristic which distinguishes humanistic athletic leaders from their colleagues is their capacity to truly listen to and hear the athlete, to clearly perceive what the athlete is saying, to comprehend the hidden messages conveyed, and to discern the covert agendas within the player's communication. In the humanistic setting, quite often the coach does not like what he/she hears. In any case, however, the coach affords the athlete's respect and treats them with the dignity which all people deserve, contemplates the athlete's thoughts, and composes a response. Regardless of whether the athlete and coach agree or are in conflict concerning a particular issue, humane treatment, consisting of respect for the athlete's person and views and a response which supports the dignity and worth of the athlete is required. The humanistic coach can criticize or disagree with the performer without losing respect for the participant, without creating unnecessary self-doubt or undo anxiety in the athlete, and without diminishing the performer's self-esteem.

COGNITIVE PROCESSES

Athletic programs designed in accordance with humanistic precepts attempt to establish a climate in which participants are cognitively as well as physically involved in sporting endeavors. In essence, athletes are placed in situations which require utilization of cognition and other cognitive abilities as well as psychomotor skills. Experiences are structured for athletes to: (1) make decisions, (2) understand and learn rules, strategies, tactics, etc., and (3) comprehend the complex physiological and mechanical nature of the physical skills in their games. In every case, high-level cognitive functioning, requiring evaluation, analysis, and/or synthesis, is emphasized, with a concomitant de-emphasis on memorization and rote learning.

The coach respects the athlete's ability to think and fully anticipates that he/she will utilize this ability in his/her efforts and decision making. The humanistic coach, well aware of the unique and subjective nature of people, respects the result of such cognitions, even though such freedom often results in disagreement, divergent thinking, and conflict. Among the goals of the humanistic coach is the fostering of the athlete's independence and does not include the reinforcement of athletes who mimic or replicate the thinking and views of the leader. Humanistic sport endeavors are designed to minimize the nurturance of dependent, acquiescent, or fawning athletes.

Within a humanistic athletic framework, cognitive activity occurs and is emphasized concurrently with psychomotor practice. The humanistic sport phenomenon is characterized not only by physical practice but also by self-analysis; introspective assessments of the athlete's own performance; formal and informal evaluations of team performance; individual, long- and short-term goal setting; individual and team training regimes, etc. The list of such cognitive possibilities is long, as well as personally relevant to the sport experience. Yet, the exact nature of such activities is secondary to the emphasis placed on the process of cognition via the sport experience.

Another aspect of humanistic coaching behavior which emphasizes the athlete's growth in the area of cognitive abilities relates to the participant's concentration. Humanistic coaches are concerned about the athlete's ability to control their focus during performance. They take steps to prepare athletes to take control of their cognitions so that the athlete performs without too much attention focused on the coach's needs, directions, instructions, etc. Humanistic coaches try to develop athletes who are able to clearly focus on their role within the environment of competitive sport, and are liberated from cognitively controlling his/her motor behavior. In effect, then, coaches attempt to develop performers who are able to transcend control of the mind. According to Gallwey (1974), in his classic work, *The Inner Game of Tennis,* athletes know intuitively that "their peak performances never come when they're thinking about it" (p. 7). It is to this level of performance that coaches attempt to bring their athletes. It is suggested here that a humanistic approach to coaching will facilitate the achievement of this goal.

CONGRUENCE

Just as a humanistic program of sport expects athletes to be real and genuine, so too is it anticipated that coaches will be authentic. The authentic personality is characterized by openness and honesty. Sport conducted within a humanistic framework provides the coach with the freedom to be spontaneous, expressive, and responsive. He/she has many opportunities for self-discovery, self-learning, exploration, and experimentation, just as he/she helps create such circumstances and happenings for the athletes. The coach is free to be him/herself.

To be authentic, a coach must respond to athletes as humans and rightfully expect the same consideration from athletes. The humanistic coach would be secure enough to respect the autonomy of others, and he/she would appreciate that athletes have their own purposes to fulfill.

The tendency of most coaches is to show themselves to athletes as individuals simply filling a role. Using such a facade, coaches fill or play the role of the coach, complete with whistle and cap. In the humanistic setting, however, the coach is secure enough to share anger, frustration, fear, etc., with the athletes. The coach, in effect, is not put off by the effects of revealing personal and subjective feelings, thoughts, emotions, etc., to the athletes. A humanistic coach can reveal his/her human self and still not feel threatened nor feel that he/she has lost face with the team.

A major characteristic of authentic individuals is their general refusal to accept stereotypical roles within society. To be authentic, a coach must first be liberated from the prevailing coaching stereotype. A humanistic coach would resist putting on his/her "game face"; would reject outright the macho, insensitive, roughneck image; and would scoff at the "general-in-command-of-the-troops" depiction of the athletic leader.

Rather, the coach would be true to his/her own ideals and to his/her own personality, feelings, emotions, and subjectivity. Within a humanistic context the coach is not the supreme leader, all-knowing, all-wise, forever good. The coach, instead, is human, one who errs, loses his/her temper, with likes and dislikes as well as personal needs.

Humanistic sport, then, requires that the coach not be stifled in his/her progress toward fulfilling his/her potential. If this is the case, then the coach will find it easy to be real and genuine. Humanistic sport assists and encourages the pursuit of maximal development and self-actualization by both athletes and coaches. The authentic coach is in the process of becoming fully aware and fully functioning in much the same manner that the athlete is.

The freedoms happily furnished the athlete in no way should impinge on the personal liberties of the coach. Theirs is an egalitarian partnership in the athletic endeavor. The authentic coach realizes that his/her athletes do not exist for his/her own self-enhancement. Neither the athlete nor the coach should fill their needs at the expense of the other.

Coaches should accent the social lives of their athletes within an atmosphere which encourages all to be authentic and genuine. This facet requires the coach to be non-judgmental about the feelings and opinions expressed by athletes. Coaches must be honest and open. Concurrent with these behaviors, coaches must take steps which clearly allay the athletes' fears of reprisals for such openness and honesty.

In sport there exists the problem of the "coachable athlete," that is, the athlete who misrepresents his/her experience and him/herself in order to produce a more attractive image to the coach. The athlete, in this case, attempts to protect him/herself. Athletes will disclose their true being and the way they view the world only to those whom they trust. Without such trust, athletes will conceal or misrepresent their experience, hoping to deceive the coach and lead him/her to a manufactured and calculated image of the athlete (Jourard, 1968).

Another aspect of congruent behavior relates to the agreement between actions and words. Coaches must be aware of the often dual messages emitted in their interactions with athletes. Heitmann and Kneer (1976) state that: "Non-verbal messages often communicate feelings which reinforce or contradict what is said verbally. . . . People tend to believe behavior—which is harder to hide" (p. 70).

Although the coach would be accepting of individuals and would always try to understand the athlete's behavior, this does not mean endorsement of inappropriate behavior. The principles of humanistic sport require an acceptance of the athlete, which may or may not include acceptance of the athlete's behavior. The genuine, honest coach would not feel uncomfortable rejecting inappropriate sport behavior.

EMPATHY

Sport structured in accordance with humanistic principles requires leadership that is sensitive to the feelings of others. Leaders of athletes who are empathic never lose sight of the experience that the athletes are undergoing. Typical of humanistic coaches is their total awareness and understanding of what it means individually and how it feels subjectively to participate in a sports program, play on a team, and to be led by a coach.

The humanistic coach realizes the importance of understanding athletes. In essence, athletes have a real and pressing need to be understood, not evaluated, not judged, simply understood from their own point of view, not the coach's. Therefore, it should be obvious that an overriding concern of and a motivating force for the humanistic coach is his/her desire to experience the athlete and his/her world in much the same way as the athlete does. This is the coach's goal, even though he/she realizes that this is truly not possible. However, efforts directed at this empathic understanding will be greatly appreciated by the athlete and will be an enlightening experience for the coach.

Empathetic behavior includes much more than friendliness or the coach's disposition toward humor, being easy, or somewhat less than a hard-nosed taskmaster. The empathetic coach encourages the athlete to express him/herself and then can respond in a sensitive manner, which reflects his/her non-judgmental stance. More importantly, the coach tries to understand the feelings and thoughts conveyed, never losing sight of the fact that such expressions are significant expressions of his/her being.

Each athlete has a physical structure, temperament, and intelligence. Generalizations regarding these aspects can be made with some confidence. However, the athlete's humaneness is a singular concoction of these attributes interacting with each other in a unique and special manner. The athlete recognizes that good coaching behavior requires an awareness of problems that athletes regularly encounter, a willingness to be tolerant and patient with the athlete's shortcomings, and an appreciation of the world of the athlete. It is unrealistic for a coach to treat all athletes alike, assuming that they all have the attributes required for success. Programs and leaders which adhere to such ideas predispose participants for failure.

Coaches must be attentive to the uniqueness of each athlete and to the singular pattern of growth and development manifested by each athlete. They must adjust the tasks of the athletic endeavor by creating an environment which will be conducive to growth and success within the sport experience.

PART III: SCENARIO NO. 1

In this first scenario the coach exhibits several humanistic behaviors. Most of the planning and organization of the practice session is carried out by the athletes. The coach goes along with the wishes of the players regarding practice, although at times he expresses views to the contrary. The coach is able to be himself and vent his disagreement without a loss of face or feeling that he has not fulfilled his coaching responsibilities.

Note also the coach's reliance upon questions to direct the drillwork as well as to encourage self-discovery and provide feedback. The use of questions also points to the coach's attention to the cognitive domain, which is another characteristic of the humanistic athletic leader.

As a final point, the reader should focus on the coach's empathic behavior and his understanding of the tedium, unpleasantness and difficulty of some drills, as well as the discouragement often felt by athletes.

A Humanistic Approach to Youth League Basketball Practice

It is 6:00 P.M. and a church team is about to commence their once-a-week, one-hour practice session. As soon as the basketball floor is cleared, ten boys 10-12 years of age scatter to the two baskets and begin dribbling, shooting, passing, and rebounding in a formation which remotely resembles a lay-up drill. These boys are inexperienced athletes, and for many it is their first organized, adult-sponsored sport experience.

The team is midway through its schedule and has a record of four wins and six losses. A fundamentally weak team, their efforts have been plagued by poor passing, weak shooting, and ineffective man-to-man defense. However, their quickness, fine rebounding, and exuberance, along with their unwillingness to give up, have stood out as team strengths.

Given the opportunity to plan their practice sessions, after much discussion, much give and take between and among players and coaches, and after several weeks, the players have decided on the following practice format:

I. 15 minutes
  1) Lay-up drill
  2) Jump-shooting drill

II. 20 minutes
  1) One-on-one defensive footwork drill
  2) Two-on-two half-court basketball

III. 25 minutes
  1) Game situations, with foul shooting (i.e. controlled scrimmage
  2) Free scrimmage, with foul shooting

Only after much diligent preparation and much patience on the part of the coach were the players ready to decide on the content of each practice. The slow, tedious, and difficult weaning process that humanistic coaches must employ to bring athletes to the point of making meaningful decisions was made more difficult by the fact that most of the athletes lacked basketball experience. It has taken this team almost half the season to reach the point of being comfortable with the decision-making process and being self-reliant in the sport setting.

Although the coach believes that the team needs to spend more time on drills emphasizing fundamentals and less time in free scrimmage, he has encouraged the athletes in their efforts to take control of their practice sessions, and the season in general. The coach does not attempt to hide his true feelings regarding the practice schedule. He freely expresses his views and discusses his concerns regarding the content of the sessions. Nevertheless, he respects the decisions that the team makes and willingly works within this format, while remaining true to his own beliefs and thereby remaining genuine and authentic.

During the 5-10 minutes of the initial two drills, both of which are organized and supervised by the young athletes themselves, the coach observed the action. Periodically, he conferred with individual athletes, often posing questions related to their techniques. The coach directed his efforts at several objectives: (1) to learn if the athlete can analyze his own performance; (2) to discover if his athletes have a complete understanding of the skills and techniques involved in basketball; (3) to assist the players in the identification of exemplary demonstrations of athletic performance; and (4) to provide encouragement and positive feedback for their efforts.

At 6:15 P.M. the coach calls the group together for a brief meeting.

COACH: Well, I'm glad to see all of you concentrating on your passing during the lay-up drill. Well done! You're all working hard. Incidentally, what were we doing in the shooting drill today that you, in general, did not do so well in last Saturday's game? (Pauses) . . . Does anyone know?

BOBBY: Look at the basket?

COACH: Well, . . . yes, we all need to look at the basket when shooting. Many of us did try to watch the rim on Saturday. Anyone else? Anybody have any other ideas?

JOHN: Follow through? I know I was trying hard to remember to completely follow through. I was trying to touch the basket with my fingers after I shot the ball.

COACH: That's it, John. Saturday, we often failed to fully flex our wrist in this way upon releasing the ball (the coach demonstrates the proper execution). Does anyone know why a shooter will often fail to follow through in a game, yet will do it in practice?

BOBBY: Yes, I know. Because of the defensive player.

COACH: Yes, that's right. Often, because of the defensive player's hand action, the shooter modifies his shot. Very often this means a missed shot. Well done, Bobby. For those of you who questioned why we usually practice shooting with at least some token defense, well, Bobby just provided you with an excellent reason. Good thinking, Bobby.

COACH: Okay, let's go into our one-on-one defensive drill. We've done this before. Does everyone remember it? (Group responds positively, albeit, unenthusiastically and with some moaning and groaning.) Okay, okay, I know you can't stand this drill. I didn't like it either as a player. It's difficult and hard work, and it hurts, too! It's up to you. You decided to work on it. What do you say gang?

TEAM: (Altogether) Alright, alright, we'll do it.

COACH: Good. Remember, defensive player keep your hands behind your back. Do not reach in. Play defense with your legs. The offensive player just try to beat the defensive man. If you do, however, stop, let him catch up. Then start again. Okay, spread out. Let's have five pairs.

The team quickly and efficiently divides into five dyads and commences with the drill. Bobby works with John. The coach observes and notes that each time Bobby is on offense, John is able to keep his body between the ball and the basket. However, when the boys switch roles, John goes by Bobby every time. Bobby, although somewhat irritated and discouraged, says nothing.

The coach signals both boys to him.

COACH: Why does John continually get by you, Bobby? What's going on here?

BOBBY: I'm not sure. I'm watching his belt buckle and I'm not following his fakes. Yet, everytime he switches left to right or right to left on his dribble, he beats me.

COACH: John, can you help? Can you explain your ability to get by Bobby?

JOHN: I think so. For some reason, when I move quickly right then left, Bobby crosses his feet. Then, it's easy to go by him.

COACH: Right! Good analysis. Now, how do we help Bobby? (Pauses to think) Let me see, . . . Bobby, go on offense. John, take your defensive stance. Now, Bobby, try to go by him.

Bobby tries to do this several times. Each time he is unable to get by John.

COACH: Stop! Bobby, look at John's defensive stance. Is it the same as yours? Different? Look carefully.

Bobby observes John's defensive stance. He looks puzzled. He appears to be deep in thought. A few moments pass.

COACH: Okay, Bobby, try again. This time attend carefully to John's defensive stance.

Bobby attempts, yet fails to get by the defensive player.

COACH: Okay, is there anything that John does that you don't do?
BOBBY: I can't see anything, coach.
COACH: Okay, switch. Bobby you go on defense. Check your stance. John, look at Bobby's stance. Tell us what you see. Do you notice anything significant?

JOHN: Well, coach, I don't think I stand up as high as Bobby does. Would that make a difference?

COACH: Let's see. Try to go by Bobby.

John proceeds to go by Bobby, easily, five consecutive times. Bobby looks down at his feet.

COACH: Bobby, don't get down on yourself now. I know you feel terrible. Try making an adjustment. Focus on John's position. I know you can do it. (Pauses) Maybe John can help.

JOHN: Bobby, get down lower, like I do.

The boys continue with the drill. Bobby seems to improve. Once in a while he prevents John from getting by him (i.e. keeps his body between John and the basket).

COACH: Much better, Bobby. That's the way to work. (Pauses to observe) . . . Okay, boys, what does the height of the defensive stance have to do with good defense?

BOBBY: I'm not sure, but I seem to get my legs tangled much more the straighter and taller I am on defense.

COACH: You're on the right track.

JOHN: It seems like it takes Bobby longer to react to my moves the higher up he is. Could that be it, coach?

COACH: I think so, John. Excellent. Remember, there is a relationship between stability and mobility.

Bobby, excited, interrupts the coach.

BOBBY: I remember! Yes, mobility decreases as you increase stability, and vice-versa, right, coach? I'm probably off balance because I'm too tall in my defensive stance. Does that sound right, coach?

COACH: Yes. Beautiful. So, in effect, Bobby, the reason offensive players can go around you is this — your elevated position on defense makes you too mobile. After a good fake or feint by the offensive player, it is easy for you to overreact and you quickly lose your balance, causing you then to take more time to regain the proper defensive stance. By that time the offensive player has gone by you. Understand?

John and Bobby affirm this together.

COACH: Well done! Now let's get to work.

PART IV: SCENARIO NO. 2

There are several significant humanistic behaviors manifested by the coach in this second scenario. The softball coach here attends to the athlete's subjective interpretations of the sport experience by means of the individual conference. In these meetings, the coach encourages self-evaluation. An important corollary to this latter behavior is the coach's avoidance of social comparison and evaluations in public as well as assessments by the coach.

Note also the group decision-making process established by the coach. At times, the coach yields to the athletes' desires and, after expressing her dismay at their decision, abides by their wishes. In effect, the coach can be open and genuine with her athletes.

The coach also encourages the athletes to generate significant input into the nature, content, and organization of the practice sessions as well as competitive game play. Note also the coach's careful preparation of her players to take charge of the action during game play.

Finally, readers should not overlook the coach's demonstration of empathy for the athletes as well as her willingness to accommodate for individual differences.

A Humanistic High School Softball Practice

It is 3:00 P.M., Wednesday, the day after ABC high school defeated XYZ high school. Though early in the season, ABC has showed much promise. This practice is in preparation for the next contest scheduled for Friday.

During the first twenty minutes of practice a variety of activities take place. The female athletes straggle in and take part in general-conditioning activities, initiated by the athletes themselves. Several athletes jog around the field, others are sprinting across the outfield. Then the athletes warm up by playing catch or playing pepper with teammates. At some point during this seemingly informal phase of practice, the coach meets individually with each athlete. During this conference the athlete and the coach review the athlete's analysis of her most recent performance. Initially, the coach simply listens to the athlete. Occasionally, the coach interjects a question, usually to clarify the athlete's thought or to facilitate the self-analysis. At no time does the coach evaluate or judge the athlete's performance. Her objective is to assist the individual in her effort to clearly understand her performance, to know herself, and to identify the athlete's strengths and weaknesses, all intended to facilitate the identification of relevant, appropriate, and personal objectives for the practice sessions of the week. Once the athlete has concluded her introspective analysis, the coach comments upon the athlete's perception and accuracy of her analysis, again avoiding comparative judgment of the individual's ability. At this point, the coach may refer to her notes, that she recorded during the last game.

Each athlete, in turn, meets with the coach in this fashion, until the entire group of twenty or so members has done so. This has become a regular feature of the first scheduled practice session after a competitive event.

When the coach has met with everyone, the team is called together to analyze yesterday's game and to discuss the plans for today's session. After several minutes of animated discussion, the group decides to work on the two major weaknesses of the team as identified by the players (both were recurrent themes in the coach-athlete conferences held at the beginning of practice). The identified weaknesses are: (1) coverage of first base by the pitcher on a ball hit to the right of the first baseman, and (2) throws from the outfield to the "cut off" player, specifically on throws to third base.

While the coach would prefer working on these skills as a group, one at a time, she yields to the team's desire to practice both at the same time. The team expresses the view that the drills do not require the involvement of all the players simultaneously, and also that time will be conserved, thereby leaving more time for the group's favorite activities (that is, batting practice and the simulated practice game). After expressing her dissatisfaction with their suggestion and informing the team that she believes the team would be better off if all the athletes would learn and practice the intricate maneuvers required in these situations, she acquiesces. In effect, she permits the athletes to direct the nature of the practice session.

The team now divides itself into two groups (outfielders, shortstops, and third baseman in one group; pitchers, catchers, first and second basemen in another). The coach does not directly lead any activity but, rather, observes and offers suggestions when help is requested. In other words, the drills are organized and administered by the players themselves. There is a flurry of self-directed, motivated activity in each group as they attend to the tasks of their particular drill. Often, the coach directs questions to individual players. These queries focus on the player's understanding of her actions as well as involving the player cognitively in the motor activities. Consequently, the athletes develop increased awareness of the situation, improved motor skills, and enhanced knowledge of the game in general.

During this thirty-minute time span, the coach also has the opportunity to discuss the game plans with the two designated captains for the next game. Questions regarding lineup formation, assignment of positions, use of substitutes, rule interpretations, strategic decision making, etc., are discussed to the satisfaction of the two players who will have such responsibilities at the next game. The coach also poses several hypothetical situations to these youngsters which generates more questions and continued discussion. In this way, the coach prepares the athletes to truly take control of their game.

Although the coach will sit with the team on the bench, her role is minimized during game play. Basically, she will serve as a resource for the two captains during the game. Also, she actively notes and sometimes records her specific observations about the athletes' performance during the game. These notes are brought to the next practice and utilized in the individual conference with athletes.

The coach now returns to the ongoing drills, which are drawing to a close. She directs a question to Susan, after observing that several throws from the outfielder pass over her head and yet land wide of the third baseman.

COACH: Susan, why are you standing in that particular spot?

SUSAN: I'm not sure.

COACH: Think about what you are doing. What is your purpose when in the cutoff position?

SUSAN: I think I'm supposed to help the outfielder line up her throw as well as to catch the ball if the third baseman tells me to, and to be ready to throw someplace.

COACH: Well said, Susan. Correct. Now, look at where you are. Can you do those things well where you are standing?

SUSAN: No, not really. Well, not both. I can catch the ball, but I'm not certain my position helps the outfielder to aim her throw.

COACH: Excellent! Your analysis is right on target. Now, see if you can make the necessary adjustments. Look around. Who could help you get to the proper position?

Susan thinks, looks around and quickly moves to a new position.

COACH: Much better, don't you think? How did you come to this new position? Where should you seek help during the game?

SUSAN: Well, I think the third baseman can help me move into a better position.

COACH: Yes. Right. Try it again.

A throw from the outfielder passes directly over Susan and travels directly to third base.

SUSAN: Yes, I see what you mean. Thanks.

The coach continues observing throughout the drillwork in this manner, directing questions which foster awareness, cognitive growth, as well as enhancing motor performance. The intent of these actions is to encourage the athlete to think, to make decisions, to become more consciously aware of her behavior. The coach offers assistance in an indirect facilitative manner rather than in an authoritative or autocratic way. In this way the athletes come to depend upon their own abilities and judgment for direction, rather than looking to and becoming dependent upon the competencies and wisdom of the coach.

The next drill is the game-situation drill. There is a player at every position, including the pitcher. Game-like situations are created by the extra players hitting the ball, running bases, etc. The team in the field must react, make decisions, and, in effect, play as if in a ball game. Again, the coach moves about the field questioning, probing, and discussing with the players their decision-making techniques, levels of awareness, etc. The coach attempts to assist the athletes in their understanding of, and their development of, motor skills in the intricacies of their position and the game.

Periodically, the coach calls out for the athletes to rotate to new positions, to move into or out of the field, or to become runners or serve as batters. The team works on this drill for thirty minutes.

Batting practice is scheduled for the next thirty minutes. This always generates excitement and animated exuberance, since the athletes love to bat. The team quickly forms six or seven triads (i.e. batter, pitcher, and fielder). For several minutes the athletes are quite involved, so the coach goes from batter to batter, silently watching. This continues until Mary, batting right-handed, calls for help.

MARY: Coach, I stink. I can't hit today! Help!
COACH: Hang in there, Mary. You don't stink! What seems to be
           the problem?
MARY: If I knew I wouldn't have called you!
COACH: Take it easy, Mary. I realize that you're having a rough
           time and you're annoyed at yourself, but try to stay calm.
           What is the problem?
MARY: I don't know. Everything I hit goes to the second base side
           of the infield.

COACH: Yes, I've noticed. Have you tried to analyze why this is occurring?

MARY: Yes.

COACH: Okay, let me hear what you think.

MARY: Well, I think my weight is equally distributed over my feet. Shirley doesn't think I'm stepping to right field. I'm not stepping into the bucket, either. My stride seems to go straight to the pitcher. Oh, I just don't know.

COACH: Mary, calm down. Don't get down on yourself. Last game you got two hits for us, right? I know you feel confused and frustrated at this moment, but don't let these feelings destroy your confidence or divert your concentration. Maintaining concentration is an important part of hitting. You're a good hitter, Mary. You've always hit well. Together, we'll work this out. Let me watch you hit a few more pitches.

MARY: Okay, here goes.

Mary hits ten more pitches. Seven of the ten dribble weakly to the second base side of the infield. She is now obviously irritated and agitated.

MARY: See what I mean, coach?

COACH: Yes, Mary. Take your batting stance. Get ready, as if you were about to hit the ball. Can you tell me what the top end of the bat is doing?

Mary assumes her batting position. A concerted look appears on her face, indicative of intense concentration.

MARY: I don't know? It feels okay to me.

COACH: Come on, relax. Concentrate. You'll see what I'm driving at. Try to feel it. Concentrate on the end of the bat, its position, its movement, and its feel. Concentrate. You can do it.

Mary continues to concentrate as she returns to batting several more pitches.

MARY: Can it be? Am I moving the bat?

She hits three more pitches.

MARY: Okay, yes, I feel it, I think. Am I moving the bat?

COACH: Yes, ever so slightly. Just prior to initiating your swing. How does that relate to hitting balls to the second base side of the infield?

MARY: Well, it's a motion I'm not sure I need. Does it slow me
            down in my rush to bring the bat to the ball? . . . Oh no!
            It probably ruins my timing!

COACH: Yes, I think that's it. Well done! Try now to control the
            bat. Try to remove the extra "jiggle" that you do just prior
            to moving the bat to the ball.

Mary continues batting, working hard to correct the flaw in her batting.
The entire team continues batting for thirty minutes. At that point the
coach calls time and suggests commencing the simulated game. Moans
and groans arise from the group. It's obvious that the athletes are enjoying the batting practice.

ALICE: (Approaching the coach) Coach, can't we bat a bit longer?
            Please?

COACH: (A look of consternation appears on her face) Alice, if we
            continue batting, we'll have to shorten the practice game
            or extend practice a few minutes. Personally, I'd rather
            not extend practice.

BARBARA: Oh, coach, let's have a longer batting practice. I'll stay a
            few minutes longer for practice. How about it? Who else
            wants to stay and practice batting a bit longer?

Most of the athletes excitedly voice their agreement, drowning out the few
who object. Reluctantly, the coach agrees. Cheers arise from the group.
Batting practice continues for several more minutes. The coach approaches
those few athletes who cannot remain at practice for the additional time
and she works out individual arrangements to accommodate their needs.

A bit later the group forms two teams, each one directed by one of
the designated captains for the next game. During the practice game
which follows, the coach directs most of her attention to these two athletes. She responds to their inquiries about making strategic, tactical
and personnel decisions during the game. Also, during this part of the
practice, the coach individually addresses the concerns of individual
players related to specific game situations that may arise.

PART V: HUMANISTIC COACHING
BEHAVIOR—SPECIFIC EXAMPLES

In this section specific behaviors, suggestions, and situations are outlined that will provide the reader with examples of humanistic coaching.

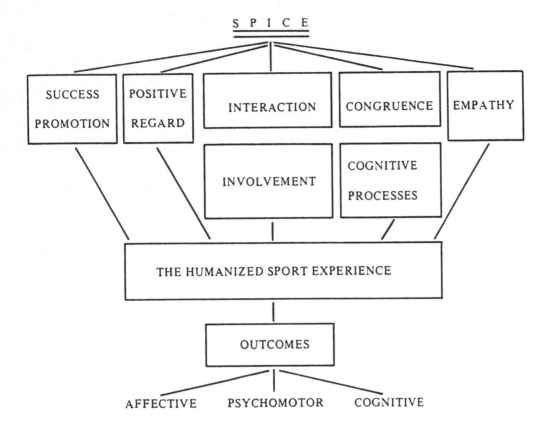

Figure 1. The Humanistic Model of Sport

In contrast with the scenarios previously described, these suggestions are presented out of context, as such, in the hope of providing as broad and varied a range of coaching behaviors as possible. The specific behaviors are derived from the S-P-I-C-E model depicted in Figure 1. Starting with the individual components of the model, coaching behaviors and situations were generated, all of which attempt to demonstrate the application of humanism to sport. In this way, the unlimited potential of the humanistic approach to sport and athletic coaching will be more readily visualized.

Success Promotion — Athletes' Goals Count, Too

1. The coach should consult with experienced team members and discuss their personal needs and desires for the upcoming year. Individual and personal goals should be identified and established based on the results of these conferences.

2. Conferences should be conducted regularly with individuals and the team as to the specific conduct of practice sessions. The intent of such consultation would be to insure that there is congruence between the individual athlete's goals and the plans for practice sessions.

3. The coach should confer with the athlete regarding his/her goals for the sport season, on a regular basis, for several reasons. It is one of the tasks of the coach to assist the athlete in identifying realistic as well as personally revelant goals.

4. On a regular basis throughout the sport season, the coach should discuss with athletes their progress toward their goals. Part of the process of promoting success relates to the periodical assessment of the athlete's goals. On occasion, it may be necessary to revise some, disgard others, and create additional goal statements. In no case does the coach impose his/her personal or team goals on the performer.

5. The evaluation process within humanistic sport mandates that the coach assess the athlete's performance on the basis of the performer's goals and avoid comparative evaluation procedures and externally generated standards. At all times the coach focuses on the individual's experience. In some cases the coach must assist the athletes in modifying their definition of success, which typically is interpreted as winning championships, performing well, enhanced motor proficiency, selection to all-star teams, and trophies.

Coaches sometimes have to help athletes modify their personal interpretation of athletic success to include additional indicators of success (e.g. number of at-bats, minutes played, positions played). The adjusted definition of success would have many implications for the humanistic coach's efforts at promoting success, since the process includes the identification of personal goals.

6. The coach needs to emphasize the development of skills related to the anticipated self-evaluation procedures, which the coach will ask the athlete to employ periodically throughout the season. This means that the coach must instruct, guide, and nurture such abilities in the athlete. Of special note are those athletes not accustomed to such self-analysis, performers new to sport, and experienced athletes who have never encountered humanistic practice within athletic organizations.

7. The process of preparing athletes to independently determine goals of the sport experience as well as the processes of self-analysis may require much work on the part of the athletic coach. The humanistic coach must not only prepare the athlete for such experiences but must also be ready to encourage, nurture, and support such efforts. The ex-

perience of self-evaluation is not easy. The coach must be patient and provide assistance where and when necessary. Rogers (1969) supports such practice and believes that if the athlete is to become independent and self-reliant, "he must be given opportunities at an early age not only to make his own judgments and his own mistakes but to evaluate the consequences of these judgments and choices" (p. 163).

8. Another aspect of success promotion relates to the avoidance of future conflicts between participation in sport and other aspects of the performer's life. Here, the coach should discuss and establish with athletes the procedures to be employed when the athlete's responsibilities to the team conflict with demands emanating from the athlete's family commitments, social life, work problems, etc. Such actions will insure that all understand the procedures established co-jointly and will minimize confusion and possible disenchantment.

9. Coaches should allow and expect many trials for an athlete to master a task. They should not keep track of trials, failed attempts, or similar statistics. Rather, athletic leaders should appreciate the small steps achieved and gradual progress made by athletes (Cox, 1985).

10. A coach can promote success by keeping track of an athlete's successes and focusing on, emphasizing, and applauding them.

11. Coaches also must focus on the athlete's skills and capabilities, rather than on their weaknesses. By stressing what the athlete can do, the coach will continually reinforce the athlete's belief in him/herself. Such psychologically constructive behavior will reap many benefits, as well as build a positive athletic climate.

Positive Regard — Coaches Value Athletes

1. The coach must convey to the athletes the fact that they have value much greater than their value as athletic performers. The humanistic coach takes great interest in the athlete's world and expresses concern about the athlete's schoolwork, social behaviors, family problems, career interests, and employment. Although some coaches will express interest in such aspects only because these items can influence the athlete's performance, truly humanistic athletic leaders are interested in the whole athlete and take measures to insure that the athletes perceive this message. Some coaches extend such interest for the duration of the coach-athlete relationship only. Once the athlete's eligibility has been exhausted, the personal interest and concern expressed by the coach disappears. Such coaches extend such attention for the purpose of controlling

the athlete, rather than simply appreciating the performer for who and what they are as an individual.

A measure of such coaching behavior and whether it is sincere or not will be the number of ex-athletes who return to visit the "old coach." Coaches who are truly and sincerely interested in the whole athlete, experience an never-ending stream of past competitors returning to visit with them, for they know that the person who is the coach is interested in them as people, not only as athletes. While such behavior by itself does not make a coach wholly humanistic, it is a humanistic characteristic and indicates that the potential for humanizing the sport experience is well within reach of such a coach.

2. Another facet of positive regard relates to the method of providing feedback or information about the athlete's performance to the athlete. The humanistic coach attempts and prefers to use an indirect method of providing performance feedback. That is, the coach will ask a question so that the athlete must analyze and think for him/herself rather than provide the performer with the answer. Notice in this next example how the coach forces the athlete to examine his/her own motor behavior before attempting to answer the athlete's inquiry.

ATHLETE: Coach, I'm missing my foul shots. The ball keeps hitting the front of the rim. What am I doing wrong?

COACH: Let's see if you can figure it out. As you practice your foul shooting, concentrate on your arm movements. Try to determine what your shoulder, elbow, forearm, wrist, and fingers are doing. That will provide us with a good start in determining the causes of your poor shooting.

3. The use of questions to provide feedback conveys several messages to athletes. First, it asserts the coach's trust and faith in the performer's ability to complete such a difficult task. The coach, in effect, is expressing his/her belief that the athlete has the capacity for such mental behavior. Second, such humanistic coaching behavior demonstrates that the answer the athlete seeks lies within the athlete. The coaching behavior here is working to eventually liberate the athlete from external control and replace it with the performer's subjective, personal, and unique control over his/her own behavior. Such behavior indicates to performers that they are the most important in the sporting endeavor and that their development is much more critical than coaches displaying their expert knowledge. In effect, such behavior suggests to the athlete that eventually he/she should become a

productive, mentally capable, and self-reliant individual independent of the coach.

4. The humanistic coach always separates the athlete's performance from the athlete's person when providing feedback. During the evaluation process, the coach addresses the overt behavior and motor performance, not the individual at hand. A coach might say, for example, after observing a poorly executed play:

> "Mary, that was a very poor pick. I know you know how to do it. Turn you body fully to insure blocking off the defense. Come on, try it again."

In this way, again, the coach expresses his/her high positive regard for the person who is the athlete. Feshbach and Weiner (1982) state that "the individual needs the experience of *unconditional positive regard,* of being valued for oneself regardless of the degree to which specific behaviors are approved or disapproved" (p. 157). The coach who acts in this manner manifests behavior which informs the athlete that during participation in sport the behavior of concern is the athletic one, and that poor performance by the athlete should not be interpreted to mean that the player is less of a person.

5. When assisting the athlete's motor endeavors, the humanistic coach prefers to use questions. It is not intended that the coach insist on such methodology, especially if the athlete is unaccustomed to such an approach. Assuming that the coach is flexible and can radiate various coaching behaviors, the athletic leader must, at certain points in and with certain athletes, provide evaluative information about the performance. However, the humanistic leader employs this approach as little as possible and will do everything possible to provide the individual with experiences to nurture the development of self-evaluative skills.

6. Whether dealing with a star athlete or a poor performer, the coach treats everyone with respect and dignity. Again, this is an example of the coach prizing each individual, first, for their uniqueness, their subjectivity, and their humanness, and second for their athletic prowess. Regardless of their specific ability level, all within the humanistic sport setting are respected, valued, and prized for their unique human abilities and singular personality. The humane coach is able to perceive and accept each athlete in his/her own right, without the urge to classify, compare, or categorize the individual.

7. When conferring with athletes about their self-analyses, the coach encourages the athlete to initiate the evaluation procedure. Then, the

coach indicates to the athlete how effective his/her self-analysis was (i.e. was it complete, fair, accurate, perceptive, etc.). Then, if and when the coach decides to provide the athlete with evaluative comments, the coach measures the athlete's performance against the athlete's pre-determined, personal, and subjective goals. The humanistic coach prefers not to compare athletes with other athletes, finding it distasteful to compare individual athletes to objective, externally generated standards of athletic performance. These type of judgments should be left to the individual performer to impose on him/herself. The humanistic coach objects to such procedures, because they focus on external standards and are often unrelated to the goals established by the athlete.

8. Within a humanistic environment the athlete should be "encouraged to find his uniqueness, his gift" (Hellison, 1983, p. 61). In this effort, the coach needs to assist the athlete as he/she discovers him/herself and confronts his/her special talents as a human. Not only will this convey the coach's high regard for the athlete, but it will also facilitate the athlete's self-awareness and full development (i.e. progress towards self-actualization).

9. The coach responds to the goodness or positive aspects of the athlete and his/her behavior in the situation first. The coach tries to recognize and emphasize the goodness in others. A specific example here should clarify this point.

A coach has just observed a poorly executed forehand stroke by a poorly skilled tennis player. Notice several things in the following example. First, the coach recognizes the parts of the skill executed *well* by the novice player, conveying this information prior to elaborating on the poorly executed aspects of the stroke. Second, the coach attempts to complete this interaction without diminishing the athlete's motivation or self-esteem and attempts to separate the performer from the performance.

COACH: Ann, you held the racquet in the proper position and with a firm grip. Great work! You also stepped into the ball, bringing your body weight fully into the stroke. Well done! Now, can you tell me what part of your stroke needs improvement? Did you feel what went wrong during the stroke?

10. The athletic leader must always respect the individual's potential. This action is fundamental to humanism, since it remains forever optimistic about people and their ability to grow, change, and develop. In the sporting endeavor, this means that the coach must consistently

convey the idea that every player can achieve, can do better, and will do better. In short, this suggestion means that a coach can never give up on an athlete.

11. The behavior of a humanistic coach is characterized by a high positive to negative feedback ratio, even though the coach does not refrain from negative comments. In actuality this means (based on the results of recent studies by Lombardo 1982, Lombardo & Pearlman, 1984, and Lombardo et al., 1984) that for each negative response given to athletes, the coach should emit approximately six or seven positive comments about the athlete's performance (i.e. a ratio of seven to one). In practice, a coach who manifests such a ratio will find that the infrequent negative comments will be more significant, simply because it will be a rare coaching behavior. While the coach should not employ a high rate of negative comments, because of the obvious negative effect it will have on the atmosphere of sport, coaches much respond negatively in certain situations. The main point here is that the negative responses to the attempts of athletes must be employed constructively and within a context of a positive team climate (i.e. an atmosphere dominated by praise, encouragement, and optimism).

Involvement — Athletes Get Excited

1. The humanistic coach confers with the team and with individuals regarding aspects of practice sessions such as the duration, frequency, time of day, etc. These decisions should emerge from and be determined by a discussion which includes all involved individuals.

2. Together, the coach and the athletes should determine the specific content of practice sessions to insure that both group and individual goals are addressed. For example, athletes and coaches together should decide the specific objectives of the daily practice session, the specific skills to be practiced, the length of time for each drill, etc.

3. The conduct of tryout sessions is a topic which can be addressed with the veterans of the team. The coach should solicit the performer's ideas about how to best conduct these sessions, including the role and expectations of the returning players, specific skills to be demonstrated, performance standards, etc.

4. The formation of the team's schedule of contests is a subject, again, which should be discussed and resolved, based upon the efforts of the coach, players, and the pertinent administrators.

5. Athletes should assist in the identification and determination of training rules, as well as penalties for violations of same. This will occur only in an atmosphere of openness and honesty, which must be constructed and maintained by the coach.

6. The physical training regime and conditioning programs should focus on the individual needs of the players, within the format of the team. Individual athletes should be consulted and the conditioning program should be established in light of their personal goals.

7. The team and the coach should discuss bench behavior during game play to determine what the goals of such behavior should be and how best to facilitate such behavior.

8. The determination of offensive, defensive, and specific-situation strategies also should be the result of a coordinated effort on behalf of players and coaches.

9. The humanistic coach should involve the players in the calling of specific plays, calling time-outs, setting offenses, etc.

10. The coach should prepare athletes to deal with officials in an effective manner. The roles of both the coaches and players should be determined in a manner that reflects the coach's respect for the players' views, yet insures respect for all participants in the competitive event, including officials.

11. The coach should remove him/herself from the immediate presence of the performers, if possible, to emphasize and heighten the athletes' involvement in the contest. It might be possible for the coach to sit in the stands with spectators, or at least move to the opposite end of the bench from the athletes. Such actions will visually demonstrate that the athletes are in charge.

12. The coach should limit his/her communications with the athletes during game play, in order to enhance the athletes' experience of decision making and "action" during the contest.

13. With few exceptions, game decisions should be made by the participants. In this case, either the team as a group can make decisions or prior to the contest a small group of athletes can be designated as leaders or captains for the contest. The designated leadership roles could be rotated week to week or game to game.

Interaction—Athletes Are Heard

1. The humanistic coach makes every effort to listen to the athletes. Every opportunity for coach-athlete and athlete-athlete interaction is grasped. Every aspect of the sport experience is open for discussion.

2. Typical humanistic coaching behavior is the asking of questions. This behavior forces athletes to think and anticipate responses. It also suggests that athletes are capable of formulating appropriate responses.

3. Humanistic coaches are reluctant to provide answers and as much as possible try to avoid filling such a role. By refusing to become the all-knowing commander-in-chief, the coach passes meaningful control to the athletes.

4. Humanistic coaches encourage and sometimes demand that athletes interact with each other to formulate a response, create an offense, scout opposing teams, etc., all in an effort to create a climate of positive interaction and an environment to stimulate cognitive growth as well. For example, the coach might ask the athletes on his/her team to discuss the following questions (Gauron, 1985) as a way of increasing athlete-to-athlete interaction, to increase sharing of ideas which might enhance motor performance, and in general to improve team cohesion:

   a. Athletes often become tired of the daily grind and routine following a specified training regime. How do you keep yourself motivated?
   b. Sometimes, athletes find themselves disagreeing with the coach or objecting to certain coaching behaviors. What is the best way to handle these disagreements?

5. Conflict is not avoided in such humanistic environments. The athletes are encouraged to become free-thinkers, independent of their leaders. It is likely that conflict will occur. Many times, the coach will not agree with the ideas, thoughts, etc., expressed by the athletes. In a humanistic climate, the coaches as well as the athletes are free to express his/her honest views. Therefore, conflict is not suppressed. Rather, it is viewed as a natural outgrowth of free expression. In every case, however, the coach affords each athlete with respect and treats them all with the dignity that all people deserve, considers the views of the performers, and responds. Regardless of whether consensus is reached or conflict arises concerning a particular issue, humane treatment is extended to all. Such humane treatment consists of respect for the individual and his/her views, and a response which supports the worth and dignity of the individual.

6. The humanistic coach can criticize or disagree with the performer without losing respect for the participant, without creating unnecessary self-doubt or undo anxiety in the athlete, without diminishing the performer's zeal for the activity, and without diminishing the performer's self-esteem. In much the same way, the performer, via the model provided by the coach, will develop and progress to a point whereby they can treat all within the sporting venture in the same manner.

7. The coach who humanizes the sport experience supports athletes in their efforts at self-analysis and encourages athletes to share such analyses with the team. This is done so as to encourage similar behavior in other team members, as well as to enhance the individual athlete's self-evaluation ability.

8. The humanistic coach can encourage interaction by arranging for the team to take its meals (pre-, post-game) together. The time spent travelling to and from events can be productive in terms athlete-to-athlete interaction. Road trips which include overnight accommodations can be especially fruitful in building relationships which often lead to meaningful interaction.

9. At the beginning of the season the coach can establish procedures whereby the athletes interview each other or respond to specific questions. This activity can be done in small groups or pairs.

10. The coach can encourage each team member to write a short autobiography and then share all or part of it with the group. This is a fine way to increase athlete-to-athlete interaction, enhance the general group tone, and build team cohesion.

Cognitive Processes — Athletes Think

1. The use of feedback comprised of questions which require athletes to compose analytical responses facilitates and emphasizes the athletes' cognitive involvement.

2. The humanistic coach builds into every motor experience attention to the cognitive domain, whether it relates to the mechancial aspects of the skill, the rules or strategies of the sport, or discussion of the official's rule interpretation.

3. Attention is centered consistently on the athletes' ability to evaluate their performance, which forces the person to regularly make cognitions related to motor performance.

4. The coach who shares such duties as scouting, formulating offensive and defensive plans, scheduling contests, practices, scrimmages, determining the exact content of practice sessions, encourages and promotes the use of the athlete's cognitive processes.

5. At regular intervals, the coach provides athletes with opportunities to evaluate team performance and to make decisions about the weaknesses of the group. The use of written feedback forms or analytical charts, for both personal and group use, might facilitate the athletes' cognitive development.

6. The coach emphasizes the why of various activities and aspects of motor skills. In these efforts the coach should attempt to convey the conceptual understandings related to the specific sport skills under consideration. For example, the coach might explain the concepts of generating force and building of momentum as he/she explains the specific aspects of the forehand stroke in tennis. The use of printed worksheets can facilitate cognitive understanding of the motor skill as well as improve the athlete's self-analysis abilities.

7. The coach encourages and supports inventiveness, creativity, original thinking, while simultaneously discouraging duplication of his/her thought processes and the mimicking of other coaches or professionals, etc. The coach recognizes that an athlete's imagination and intuition are important parts of his/her life in sport that can be shared with others (e.g. coaches, teammates, etc.) and used to think creatively.

8. Humanistic coaches attempt to organize sport so that it helps athletes improve their abilities to perceive, feel, wonder, intuit, sense, create, fantasize, imagine, and experience (Roberts, 1975). In order to achieve these objectives the coach must structure situations within sport in which athletes are required to use their imagination, creativity, and intuition. In essence, a coach who uses an indirect approach (i.e. asks many questions) and problem-solving techniques regularly will foster the development of these abilities.

9. The coach recognizes that an athlete's imagination and intuition are important facets of his/her life in sport that can be shared with others (e.g. coaches, teammates, etc.) and used to stimulate creative thinking.

10. The athlete's original or novel cognitions should be shared with others, if the participant so desires. In this way, opportunities for discussion, group and self-analysis would be provided to ascertain the value and meaning of such cognitions. Coaches can encourage athletes to maintain a sport journal. Ravizza (1986) claims that the sport journal or log can help the athlete "develop an awareness of his/her performance so that he/she can recognize appropriate mental states" (p. 159). Ravizza continues and believes that the journal can also be a place where athletes can record "feelings and the personal knowledge" about the game, teammates, coaches, etc.

11. The coach should assist the athletes to analyze their own performance after each competitive event. Hellison (1983) emphasizes the point that coaches should help athletes study their performance "what they did right, what they needed to work on" (pp. 60-61).

Congruence — Coaches Are Authentic

1. The humanistic coach can be spontaneous without feeling inhibited or concerned about losing face. On the contrary, this is not a concern, since the congruent coach is not attempting to portray the coaching stereotype but rather is simply being him/herself. The coach is free to emit expressions of him/herself without the fear of losing the respect of the athletes.

2. The coach is free to express his/her emotions as expressions of his/her real self. That is, the coach is comfortable in responding spontaneously and displaying a wide range of emotions and feelings, as well as sharing these feelings with athletes. The coach is open and honest and can reveal him/herself to athletes, rather than portraying an image of a coach.

3. The humanistic coach displays verbal and non-verbal behaviors which are congruent. This means that what the coach is saying agrees with the coach's gestures, posturing, and non-verbal expressions. Coaches who manifest congruent behaviors do not put forth dual messages, which often frustrate athletes, certainly adds to their confusion, and tends to build distrust of the coach's words. Athletes in this situation will believe the non-verbal messages conveyed by the leader's actions and not place their trust in statements made by the coach.

4. The congruent coach does not hide his/her feelings from the athletes. Since the coach separates the athlete's behavior from the athlete's person, he/she can be honest and open when commenting about the athlete's motor performance. The coach can do this without making the athlete feel poorly or feel that he/she is not valued. For example, the coach can state, "That last pitch, Bobby, was terrible!" and not lose the respect of the player or destroy his self-esteem. When an authentic, congruent climate is created, real, subjective feelings can be expressed openly and honestly, all of which nurtures the participant's growth and development.

5. The congruent coach encourages and supports athletes as they strive to be authentic, genuine, and open. The coach does this primarily by modeling such authentic behavior. In this way, the coach's behavior facilitates the athlete's movement in this direction.

6. The congruent coach does not avoid issuing negative feedback or criticism, especially in light of the fact that he/she can provide such feedback without attacking the ego or self-worth of the individual. To be consistently genuine, a coach does not inform a player that his/her performance was well done when, in fact, it was not. The congruent coach is truthful.

7. The congruent coach is able to express a wide range of emotions and feelings and expects that athletes will respect his/her subjectivity just as the coach respects the athletes' personal expressions.

8. The humanistic coach would encourage the athletes to stop "playing the role" of the athlete (usually reflecting the professional model) and start being him/herself. By exhibiting genuine, congruent behavior, the coach would assist the athletes' growth in this direction. For example, after a defeat, the coach would not expect his/her athletes to act like professionals and express anger, sadness, and obvious signs of distress, unless these were true expressions of themselves. At all times, including immediately after competition, the coach would be disturbed if he/she did not observe the athletes being genuine and real. Some athletes after competition need some quiet, personal time, others are more boisterous, and others analyze their performance continually. The point is that the coach permits, respects, and encourages athletes to be true to themselves and does not force his/her feelings or beliefs on the athletes.

9. The coach who embraces humanism would encourage expressions which are personal and subjective. For example, on a day when the team was badly beaten, Johnny had his best all-around day since he commenced playing baseball. He fielded his position perfectly and made three hits in four at-bats. Although the team lost 12-2, Johnny was happy. In the traditional sport setting, Johnny would have had to outwardly exhibit behavior which emphasized his sadness and disappointment at his team's defeat, disregarding completely his own magnificent performance. It would not be until several hours later, well after the end of the contest, that Johnny would be able to freely express his joy and revel in his accomplishments of that day, and then probably in the privacy of his home or with his close buddies. In the humanistic setting, the coach encourages and accepts such true expressions of self. The coach does not deny the performer his/her feelings and emotions, for he/she understands that these expressions are part of the athlete's person. To deny the athlete these feelings and expressions would be, in effect, to deny the individuality, the uniqueness, of that performer. Such congruent behavior is enhanced when the leader him/herself displays such authenticity.

10. Incongruent coaching behavior often can be attributed to the commonly observed differences with the encounter with sport as experienced by coaches and athletes. Many coaches were athletes of average ability and/or average physical capacities who were overachievers and extremely hard workers. These coaches behaved in this manner in order

to achieve a modicum of success and compete successfully with athletes endowed with greater physical skills and abilities. Incongruent behavior often results when a coach, who had average skills and needed to work harder and longer than the next athlete in order to accomplish anything in sport, becomes the leader of those athletes who possess greater skills and natural abilities then he did. This coach will often expect the athletes to work and practice at the levels required of him/her. On the other hand, conflict can and very often does result when the gifted athlete does not perceive the need for such intense practice and long hours of training.

The humanistic coach, aware of his/her athletes and their skill level, will consistently plan practices and training regimes with the athletes, based upon their desires and needs. The humanistic coach does not assume that the athletes require the intense, rigid, ascetic or harsh practice/training program that he/she experienced.

11. The coach is able to reveal his/her willingness to be vulnerable, and works at being transparent. As Rogers (1969) states: "There is nothing to be afraid of when I present myself as I am, when I can come forth non-defensively, without armor, just me" (p. 228).

The coach exhibits congruence when he/she can:

- admit mistakes and recognize his/her shortcomings
- acknowledge his/her deficiencies
- recognize that he/she is ignorant where she/he should be knowledgeable.

12. The humanistic coach has the inner strength to permit athletes to be separate and different from him/her.

Empathy — Athletes' Feelings Count

1. Feedback, a major task for the humanistic coach, should be given individually when the intent is to assist the individual athlete. Humanistic leaders avoid public evaluations of an athlete.

2. Humanistic coaches provide evaluations and feedback in a form that the coach him/herself, as an athlete and person, would feel comfortable receiving. In other words, humanistic sport leaders always treat athletes as they would like to be treated if they were performing.

3. When it comes to understanding athletes, the coach should not take shortcuts. The coach should understand that to attempt to know what it is like to be an athlete on his/her team requires much effort on the part of the leader.

4. The coach should convey at every opportunity the fact that as an empathic coach, he/she is trying to understand the athletes. Just the fact that the leader is attempting to know the experience of his/her athletes will not only make for a more positive team climate but will also facilitate the achievement of this difficult (probably impossible) task. While most humanists agree that teachers and coaches must make these efforts at gaining insight into the experience of their students and athletes and attempt to accept their world, they also vehemently agree that this task is impossible.

5. The coach should have the athletes analyze their behavior and feelings during a post-game conference. This should be done for the entire group (i.e. team) as well as for each participant and non-participant (as an observer). The team should analyze its actions and feelings as a group, then the individual athlete should repeat the process privately. The coach might encourage the use of a log or journal, in which the athlete may record significant feelings, happenings, experience, etc., of either a personal or group nature. In this way, the written thoughts might facilitate the athlete's self-understanding.

6. The coach should address the athlete's feelings whenever possible. The individual's feelings should be a topic of concern within the sport experience, rather than hidden or denied.

7. The coach needs to focus on the athlete's interpretations, analyses, introspective thoughts, etc., regarding his/her personal feelings, yet without prying, or necessarily knowing the athlete's feelings. In other words, the coach should facilitate the athlete's efforts at understanding, awareness, and getting in touch with his/her feelings.

8. The coach should set aside time to discuss personal meanings and feelings experienced while participating, as well as those perceived after the sporting event. This should be done to assist the athlete's exploration of the subjective experience of sport.

9. The coach should encourage and support athletes to recognize and discuss their subjective experiences. The possibility of contrasting the subjective experience with the more objective group or team experience should be explored.

10. The coach should make every effort to treat opponents as worthy competitors and valuable individuals. By modeling such behavior, the coach will assist athletes in their efforts to view the opposition as uniquely skilled individuals (as they are) who are striving to do the same as they are. In effect, the coach's behavior here will do much to combat the often senseless dehumanization of the opposition commonly encouraged and accepted within the sport world.

11. Similarly, the coach demonstrates caring and compassion for all in the sport situation, not only his/her athletes. For example, the coach applauds excellent performance, regardless of which team has executed well. The coach praises the play and skills of opposition players. The coach is concerned and assists as much as possible when opposition players are injured. Such coaching behavior will enable the athletes to identify more closely with the opposition athletes. Athletes should come to view the opponents as "extended teammates" (Sage, 1978).

12. Empathy will be developed if the coach encourages inter-team fraternization. For example, if the coach can arrange pre- and/or post-game meals for the competing teams, understanding and empathy for the opponent will be nurtured. The more contact an athlete has with the opposing players, the more respect and, more importantly, the better understanding of that opponent as a mirror image will develop.

13. Another activity that will promote understanding and empathy would be cross-team practice sessions or scrimmages. In this example, teams would be composed of performers from two or more teams. Therefore, the athletes would be placed in a situation in which they must cooperate, assist each other, and play together, all of which will facilitate understanding of the "other team" as individuals.

Chapter 5

EPILOGUE: QUO VADIS

PART I: RECAPITULATION

IN THE endeavor to discuss the potential and feasibility of humanistic athletic coaching, many relevant aspects have been addressed. At the outset, the sport experience was described and analyzed in order to formulate a realistic set of outcomes which both athletes and coaches should expect from an encounter with sport. A description of the assumptions held by the author was included, as well as the commonly stated and widely accepted contributions that sport makes to the participant's growth and development.

A brief outline of the main tenets of humanism followed that was presented to provide the reader with an introduction to humanistic psychology. This section included a review of the significant ideas of several of the major humanistic leaders, as well as a comparision of humanism with other selected psychological systems.

Next, the potential effects of a humanistic sport experience was explored. In this part of the text, the effects of humanism were analyzed from the perspective of each of the various actors in the sport setting (i.e. the athlete, the coach, and the administrator) as well as an examination of the effects of humanism on sport in general. Included here also was a cursory analysis of the factors which have mitigated against the promulgation of humanistic athletic programs.

Chapter 4 was designed to provide the reader with specific examples and suggestions of humanistic psychology applied to sport as well as to athletic coaching. Guidelines for getting started were presented followed by an explanatory analysis of the humanistic coaching model which specified the ramifications of such a system for coaching leadership.

This latter section analyzed the principles of humanism, resulting in their re-interpretation for use in sport.

This latter chapter also included two scenarios that were provided to present the reader with a more explicit and, at the same time, holistic view of humanistic sport systems. It is in these scenarios that the full flavor and meaning of humanistic coaching is conveyed to the reader. This section concluded with a list of examples of specific humanistic coaching behaviors for each principle identified. Included here also were more general suggestions and the description of possible sport situations which, if utilized, could assist the coach and other sport leaders in their efforts to humanize the sport experience. These examples are provided to further facilitate the understanding of humanism applied to athletic coaching.

At this point it would be useful to extend the present analysis to a broader, more global level. Specifically, what follows is a review of administrative changes that, if implemented, would re-focus sport from the top down.

PART II: CHANGING SPORT SYSTEMS: ORGANIZATIONAL AND STRUCTURAL MODIFICATIONS

While many of the previously described suggestions can be directed to and implemented by individual coaches acting on their own, a more effective method of fostering humanistic sport systems would be for the administration and/or organizational leaders to enforce some or all of the following modifications. A sport organization that implements the following suggestions will provide a setting that will truly support humanistic coaching endeavors thereby resulting, I believe, in a humanized sport environment.

1. Reduce funds for trophies and other tangible rewards (i.e. other extrinsic inducements for participation). By minimizing the amount of money available for such items, administrators, coaches, booster groups, parents, and fans will more readily encourage and accept intrinsic modes of reward and satisfaction. This will enhance the development of intrinsic motivation.

2. Contestants should be taught and prepared to emphasize winning only during the actual contest. When victory and winning becomes excessively important after the contest, sport becomes warped (MacKenzie, 1969). At the organizational level, this might mean restricting publicity, spectator involvement, etc.

3. Restrict or limit the coach's communications with players during the contest. This places the athlete in the position of making important, relevant, and meaningful decisions about all aspects of the game.

4. Limit practice sessions to one-and-one-half hours per day. This regulation will emphasize the point that sport is only one aspect of the individual's experience.

5. Limit the schedule of contests to one game per week. This not only de-emphasizes, somewhat, the focus on competition but also provides more time for practice and learning on behalf of the athletes. The added time is crucial in an educational sport experience, since the athletes will be prepared for much more than physical participation in the event. The additional time will be used to facilitate the development of leadership skills, instruction in appropriate decision-making strategies, motor skill analysis, etc.

6. Restrict, or eliminate entirely, scouting completed by coaches. Scouting should be, if desired, a task to be mastered by athletes as an activity which will enhance the individuals' learning related to the particular activity.

7. The organization should endeavor to maintain an atmosphere which fosters understanding of training, competition, and the sport experience. This recommendation is suggested separate and apart from a similar idea presented for the modification of coaching behavior. If the organization structures its program in this way, then coaches will find it easier to behave in this manner, which stresses a more holistic sport experience and understanding of same.

8. Athletic organizations should provide, on a regular basis, meetings, conferences, workshops, etc., for coaches, for minimally one day to events of a longer duration. Such get-togethers will encourage the sharing of ideas, experiences, techniques, etc. Such in-service activities and continual training sessions characterize all professional educational groups and should typify athletic groups, as well.

9. The meetings suggested in No. 8 above should provide for open exchange not only regarding sport but also on interpersonal relationships with athletes. Again, this practice will emphasize the experience of sport by the athlete as a holistic experience, rather than just a physical encounter.

10. Coaches should be rotated two, three, or more times during a season. In effect, this maneuver would prevent coaches from viewing any one team as "their team." In addition, all athletes would benefit from the competence and skills of all the available coaches.

11. Schedule all competitive contests during the day. This would severely restrict parents and spectators from attending and, as often happens, interfering with the play of the athletes or, by their mere presence, placing additional pressure on the performers. This would also move to minimize pressures of spectators often felt by competitors.

Organizations could schedule one or two events during the season at times when parents could conveniently attend, as a way of encouraging some parental observation and participation.

12. If possible, prepare the schedule so that contests begin after schools have closed for the summer and so that the entire season, including play-offs and the like, are concluded prior to the new school year. Although this may not be feasible in some situations, where it is possible this recommendation would alleviate pressures of several types on the athletes (e.g. athletic versus school demands).

13. If spectators are permitted, seat them at a distance from the athletes. This will also help to minimize interference and pressures which often emanate from the stands.

14. Prepare the athletes to officiate their own games. This forces athletes to truly learn their games, as well as requiring the coach to teach the athletes the rules and techniques of officiating.

15. The organization must promote various measures of success, including, but not limited to, competitiveness and victory. Success in motor ability, learning within the sport setting, and knowledge of how to be self-directed are all examples of alternative measures of success which can and should be promoted by the athletic organization as a way of encouraging the athletes to strive for other meaningful goals. In addition, it is imperative that any measure of success must include the athlete's progress toward his/her own self-determined and pre-selected goals.

16. Evaluation of performance should be completed on a more personal basis and less in relation to others (Singer & Gerson, 1980). In most athletic organizations, regardless of the individual coach's beliefs, this will only occur if the leaders stress this behavior.

17. Structure competitive situations so that participants perceive and evaluate their performance in such a manner that they are in control of their actions; their attributions should be internal rather than external (Singer & Gerson, 1980). In other words, the athletes must be taught to make rational attributions and discuss the causes of their actions in a way that will enhance their motivation for participation. Athletes must be instructed to make perceptive judgments about their ability, and coaches can do much in this vein. By insuring that athletes have per-

ceived the athletic event clearly, including their personal part in the contest, the coach can guide the athletes to realistic analyses and judgments about their sport behavior.

PART III: GAZING INTO THE CRYSTAL BALL

The future of sport will hopefully include a greater dominance of humanistic athletic leadership. The emergence of such a growth-promoting trend in sport will return sport to its roots, that is, back to its sandlot origins. In this view, suggested by several critics of sport in America (Yiannakis, 1978; Coakley, 1982), there would be minimal external intervention in the sport experience. In this way the best elements of the informal, player-organized sandlot experience would be enhanced by adding only the most positive and pertinent aspects of adult and/or externally intrusive factors.

If this situation were realized, then the following scenario might not be as far fetched as it may sound and, indeed, may someday be possible.

PART IV: SCENARIO NO. 3: PARENTS' NIGHT

In this scenario, two parents are speaking with each other.

PARENT 1: Let's go watch the kids play basketball tonight. You know this is the first of only two "parents nights" of the season. Parents are permitted to watch their children only on prescribed occasions.

At the game, the parents notice that there are very few spectators at all. There is minimal adult intervention in the activities. Actually, it is difficult to discern adult participation in the high school basketball game. The most visible adults are those stationed at the first-aid station.

PARENT 2: Even though my son said that the athletic department made some changes this year, this is not at all what I expected to see. In no way does this resemble my high school basketball experience. What is going on here?

The parents observe the following:

Athletes, in addition, who play the game will:

1. Take turns officiating the game.
2. Make all game decisions, including substitutions, offensive, and defensive strategies, etc.

3. Totally involved with the game. There are no disinterested bench warmers. There are very few substitutes at all!

4. All participants, whether playing, officiating, or sitting, seem to be enjoying themselves. Although the game appears to be as intense as ever, the players seem very relaxed as if they were playing in a pressure-free environment.

5. The coaches are within reach of the teams but are basically silent observers of the game action. The coach of one team observes quietly, periodically writing something down on his pad. A second coach speaks into a small tape recorder. Both sets of notes will be conveyed to the athletes at the next practice session.

PARENT 1: This is really strange. The coaches are not screaming out instructions. How do the players know what to do?

There are no cheerleaders, female or otherwise.

Although this is a contest between the teams with the best win-loss records, the media is not in attendance.

The athletes, with the coach present, conduct a post-game discussion and analysis. Some of the coach's notes, recorded during the contest, are utilized. By and large, the coach asks questions of the players. The discussion is animated and candid, sometimes heated, with both players and coach openly exchanging views.

Overhearing part of this exchange, parent 2 comments:

PARENT 2: Imagine that, the coach is asking questions. What's even more astounding is that the athletes are responding willingly and intelligently!

The two parents move closer to the discussion and listen in on part of the post-game analysis.

1. The coach is asking questions which cause the performers to evaluate both their individual performance and the performance of the team. The coach is not evaluating either the players or the team but rather is asking difficult questions which facilitate such analyses.

2. Athletes are offering evaluations of self and the team performance, willingly and with interest.

3. The coach is assisting the athletes with their self-evaluations, and yet is not judgmental.

4. The athletes seem not to be disturbed by the analytical process, and participate eagerly in the post-game analysis.

PARENTS: Wow! Athletics have certainly changed since we played the game.

SOME CLOSING THOUGHTS

The critical problem of sports can be summarized in the following way. Athletes initially bring intrinsic interest to the sport scene. In addition, athletes bring to athletics typical human needs of self-efficacy, achievement, competency, self-esteem, etc. (Zuger, 1952, p. 179, cited in Maslow, 1962, p. 48).

However, upon presentation to the adult leader the participant's needs become of secondary importance. The coach proceeds to do for the athlete. This is what sport is all about. Here is how you move! These are the specific techniques! Do it my way! Let me, the coach, explain the rules to you.

At this point, the interest of the participant may be unaffected. However, if the situation is examined closely, it can be observed that the athlete has little opportunity to truly get totally involved with the activity except through the direction and leadership of the coach. The athlete has minimal opportunity to match him/herself with this novel experience, except in ways defined by the coach. The athlete's process of self-discovery is hampered because it must proceed at a pace determined by others (i.e. the adult supervisor).

The actual leadership, instruction, guidance, etc., of the adult usually brings into play yet another factor. When the coach teaches skills, strategies, rules, etc., invariably there usually is an explicit expectation that the athlete will perform in a like manner (i.e. conform). Therefore, from the very outset, the athlete must focus on achieving the coach-identified objectives rather than addressing the possibility of focusing on other more meaningful, more personally satisfying, and more individually determined goals. Moreover, rarely is the athlete directed to attend to the process involved in attaining such objectives.

In addition to the goals of the coach being superimposed on him/her, the athlete must strive for such end products in an arena which includes many peers, numerous other adult leaders (assistant coaches, officials, referees, scorers, etc.) and spectators of all ages. The pressures of comparison become readily apparent, adding to external forces. Add to this Debord's (1979) claim that sport contributes little to the development of its participants, especially as regards preparation for the future, and it is easy to understand why sport administrators are "looked upon as not having creative educational plans stressing individuality or cooperation" (p. 36). Leaders of athletics, anxious to preserve the status quo, are typically conformists, anxious to maintain order and discipline. Sport programs have succeeded in "cramming techniques, win-at-all costs ideas, muscles, endurance, and discipline down the throats of our young people" (Zeigler, 1973, p. 105).

As a result, often the initial novelty of participation wears off quickly and understandably. This process is hastened, especially in circumstances in which the athlete's imagination is stifled. The performer's enthusiasm quickly wanes once the athlete realizes that he/she cannot "break out of the mechanically controlled circuit" (Heitman & Kneer, 1976, p. 9).

Authorities have emphasized that sport mirrors society. It comes as no surprise, then, that sport is dominated by leadership which clearly reflects behavioral principles. However, it is from the assumptions derived from behaviorism that sport must extricate itself if it is to truly contribute in a positive manner to the development of the athlete.

Zeigler (1973) strongly argues that sport "be administered . . . in an open, democratic manner in which the individual . . . is allowed the opportunity to achieve his or her potential, but at the same time, the welfare of all . . . being perserved" (p. 105).

Naisbett (1984) and others have argued that all aspects of society are rapidly being transformed by and becoming dependent upon technology. As society moves to rely upon "high tech," he claims that individuals will need to concern themselves with more human qualities. In his words, as society becomes more tied into high technology, there is a greater demand for "high touch" in both professional activities as well as in interpersonal relationships. In fact, Naisbett asserts that the "high-touch" skills of personal sensitivity, nurturing behavior, and facilitative interpersonal relationships may well be the critical aspect in the health and well-being of both the economy and personal wellness. Sport is by no means immune from these societal trends. Sport should be a source of "high-touch" activities. If it embraces humanism, the transition to an activity responsive to the needs of its participants would be facilitated. Sport easily could become a model of an activity which focuses on positive interpersonal relationships as a way to develop the potential of the participant.

Sport, as a form of human movement, the ultimate end of which is the growth and development of the individual, represents the form of education most able to address growth along several dimensions — psychomotor, cognitive, and affective.

Gensemer (1980) states, "It is important to note . . . that any growth-directed effort, to the extent to which it takes seriously the individual, along with his consciousness and his freedom, is in the broad sense humanistic" (p. 142).

The sport experience is truly a humanistic venture, despite the efforts by some to the contrary. Sport seriously engages the individual and has the potential to liberate the essence of being fully human. However, for sport to do this, it must provide for full participation and permit creative human expression and movement rather than staid, mechanistic movements defined by professional sport.

However, as long as sport is conducted without regard for the individual's uniqueness, subjectivity, wholeness, and innate potential and instead continues to give priority to more objective outcomes and to the products rather than the process of the sport experience, the worthy ends identified previously in this volume will never come to fruition and will remain forever ensconced within the rhetoric which abounds in sport.

Alternative coaching behavior is required to move beyond the present structure of sport, if goals of increased participation, sustained interest, enhanced mental health, and the development of an active lifestyle are to the achieved.

Humanism in sport has the potential to re-assert the personal—intuitive—subjectiveness of the sport experience. At the center of such change should be the humanistic coaching model. Athletic coaches must keep the sport experience relevant to each participant's needs and interest. The athlete must be actively engaged in and permitted responsible control of his/her sport experience in order for the athlete to explore novel experiences and pursue self-fulfillment.

The humanistic model can provide the necessary framework for such alternatives, spearheaded by humanistic coaching behavior.

As long as sport is conducted in a manner consistent with the intentions of the professional model of sport, its contributions will be greatly minimized and trivialized. Sport that is designed and administered in accordance with humanistic principles has the potential to liberate the essence of being fully human.

BIBLIOGRAPHY

Albaugh, Glenn R. "The Influence of Ressentience as Identified in College Basketball Coaches." In *Proceedings of the 75th Annual Meeting of the NCPEAM*. Minneapolis: NCPEAM, 1972, pp. 60-68.

Boyle, R.H. *Sport-Mirror of American Life*. Boston: Little, Brown, and Company. 1963.

Bressan, E.S. "Back to Basics: The Humanistic Agenda for Physical Education." In C. Ulrich (Ed.). *Education for the 80's: Physical Education*. Washington, D.C.: National Education Association, 1982, pp. 18-25.

Carron, A.V., and B.B. Bennett. "Compatibility in the Coach-Athlete Dyad." *Research Quarterly, 48:*671-679, 1977.

Cheffers, John T.F., and Thomas Evaul. *Introduction to Physical Education: Concepts of Human Movement*. Englewood Cliffs: Prentice-Hall, 1978.

Coakley, Jay J. *Sport in Society: Issues and Controversies* (2nd ed.) St. Louis: C.V. Mosby, 1982.

Cox, Richard H. *Sport Psychology: Concepts and Applications*. Dubuque, Iowa: Wm. C. Brown Publishers, 1985.

Danziger, Raymond C. "Coaching Humanistically: An Alternative Approach." *The Physical Educator, 39:*121-125, 1982.

DeBord, R.R. "Identity Crisis: Humanizing Our Sports Program." *Arena Review, 3:*33-38, 1979.

Eitzen, D. Stanley, and George H. Sage. *Sociology of American Sport* (2nd ed.). Dubuque, Iowa: Wm. C. Brown, 1982.

Ellis, M.J. *Why People Play*. Englewood Cliffs. Prentice-Hall, 1973.

Feshbach, S., and B. Weiner. *Personality*. Lexington, MA: D.C. Heath, 1982.

Fisher, A.C., V.H. Mancini, R.L. Hirsch, T.J. Proulx, and E.J. Staurowsky. "Coach-Athlete Interactions and Team Climate." *Journal of Sport Psychology, 4:*384-404, 1984.

Gallwey, W.T. *The Inner Game of Tennis*. New York: Random House, 1974.

Gauron, Eugene F. *Mental Training for Peak Performance*. Lansing, NY: Sport Science Associates, 1984.

Gensemer, Robert E. *Humanism and Behaviorism in Physical Education*. Washington, D.C.: National Education Association, 1980.

Gill, D.L., J.B. Gross, and Huddleston, S. "Participation Motivation in Youth Sports." In G.C. Roberts and D.M. Landers (Eds.): *Psychology of Motor Behavior and Sport*. Champaign, IL: Human Kinetics, 1980.

Gould, D., D.L. Feltz, and L. Petlichkoff. "Reasons for Discontinuing Involvement in Competitive Sport." *Journal of Sport Behavior, 5:*155-165, 1982.

Griffin, M.R. "An Analysis of State and Trait Anxiety Experienced in Sports Competition at Different Age Levels." *Foil, Spring:*58-64, 1972.

Heitman, H.M., and M. Kneer. *Physical Education Instructional Techniques: An Individualized Humanistic Approach.* Englewood Cliffs, NJ: Prentice-Hall, 1976.

Hellison, D. *Humanistic Physical Education.* Englewood Cliffs, NJ: Prentice-Hall, 1973.

Hellison, D. "The Magnificent Seven: High School Wrestlers Who Won While Losing." *Journal of Physical Education Recreation and Dance, 54:*60-61, 1983.

Horn, J.L., and R.B. Cattell. "Refinement and Test of the Theory of Fluid and Crystallized Intelligence." *Journal of Educational Psychology, 57:*253-270, 1966.

Jourard, Sidney M. *Disclosing Man to Himself.* Princeton, NJ: D. Van Nostrand, 1968.

Jourard, Sidney M. *The Transparent Self* (Rev. ed.). New York: D. Van Nostrand, 1971.

Lombardo, B.J. "The Coach in Action: A Descriptive Analysis." *Bulletin of the Federation Internationale D'Education Physique, 54:*9-15, 1984.

Lombardo, B.J., N. Faraone, and D. Pothier. "The Behavior of Youth League Coaches: A Preliminary Analysis." In *Studying The Teaching in Physical Education.* M. Pieron and J. Cheffers (Eds.): Liege, Belgium: International Association for Physical Education in Higher Education, 1982, pp. 189-196.

Lombardo, B.J., and C. Pearlman. "Factors Related to the Behavior of Youth Sport Coaches." Paper presented at the 1984 Olympic Scientific Congress. July 21, 1984. Eugene, Oregon.

Luschen, G. "The Interdependence of Sport and Culture." *International Review of Sport Sociology, 2:*127-238, 1967.

Mackenzie, Marlin M. *Toward a New Curriculum in Physical Education.* New York: McGraw-Hill Book Company, 1969.

Mager, Robert. "A Universal Objective." *Improving Human Performance: A Research Quarterly, 2:*181-190, 1973.

Martens, Rainer (Ed.). *Joy and Sadness in Children's Sports.* Champaign, Il: Human Kinetics Publishers 1978.

Maslow, A. *Towards a Psychology of Being.* Princeton, NJ: D. Van Nostrand, 1962.

Maslow, A. *Motivation and Personality* (2nd ed.). New York: Harper & Row, 1970.

Moriarty, D., A.M. Guilmette, and M. Ragab. "Change Agent Research." *Journal of Physical Education and Recreation, 48:*42-43, 1977.

Naisbitt, John. *Megatrends.* New York: Warner Books, 1982.

Rajeski, W., C. Danacott, and S. Hutslar. "Pygmalion in Youth Sport: A Field Study." *Journal of Sport Psychology, 1:*311-319, 1979.

Ravizza, K. "Increasing Awareness for Sport Performance." In J.M. Williams (Ed.) *Applied Sport Psychology: Personal Growth to Peak Performance.* Palto Alto, CA: Mayfield, 1986, pp. 149-162.

Roberts, T.B. (Ed.). *Four Psychologies Applied to Education: Freudian, Behavioral, Humanistic, Transpersonal.* Cambridge, MA: Schenkman Publishing Company, Inc., 1975.

Rogers, C.R. "The Interpersonal Relationship in the Facilitation of Learning." In *Humanizing Education: The Person in the Process.* Washington, D.C.: ASCD, 1967.

Rogers, C.R. *Freedom to Learn: A View of What Education Might Become.* Columbus, OH: Charles Merrill, 1969.

Sage, George H. "Machiavellianism Among College and High School Coaches." In *Proceedings of the 75th Annual Meeting of the NCPEAM.* Minneapolis, NCPEAM, 1972, pp. 45-60.

Sage, George H. "Value Orientations of American College Coaches Compared to Male College Students and Businessmen." In *Proceedings of the 75th Annual Meeting of the NCPEAM.* Minneapolis: NCPEAM, 1972, pp. 174-185.

Sage, George H. "Socialization of Coaches: Antecedents to Coaches' Beliefs and Behaviors." In *Proceedings of the 78th Annual Meeting of the NCPEAM.* University of Illinois at Chicago Circle: NCPEAM, 1975, pp. 124-132.

Sage, George H. "Humanistic Psychology and Coaching." In *Sport Psychology: An Analysis of Athlete Behavior.* William F. Straub (Ed.). Ithaca, NY: Movement Publications, 1978, pp. 148-161.

Sapp, M., and J. Haubenstricker. "Motivation for Joining and Reasons for Not Continuing in Youth Sports Programs in Michigan." Paper presented at AAHPER Convention, Kansas City, Missouri, 1978.

Shaffer, J.B.P. *Humanistic Psychology.* Englewood Cliffs: Prentice-Hall, 1978.

Siedentop, D. *Developing Teaching Skills in Physical Education.* Palo Alto, CA: Mayfield, 1983.

Singer, R., and Gerson, R.F. "Athletic Competition for Children: Motivational Considerations." *International Journal of Sport Psychology, 11*:249-262, 1980.

Ulrich, Celeste (Ed.). *Education in the 80's: Physical Education.* Washington, D.C.: National Education Association, 1982.

Ulrich, C., and LeRoy T. Walker. "Sanity in Sport." In C. Ulrich, (Ed.). *Education for the 80's: Physical Education.* Washington, D.C.: National Education Association. 1982, pp. 70-78.

Wilkerson, M., and R. Dodder. "What Does Sport Do for People?" *Journal of Physical Education and Recreation, 50*:50-51, February, 1979.

Yiannakis, Andrew. "Formal and Informal Play Settings: A Discursive Analysis of Processes and Outcomes for Children." In *Proceedings of the NAPECW/NCPEAM National Conference.* Denver, Colorado, 1978.

Zeigler, Earle F. "Women in Sport as Administrators: (or how to avoid the 'Watergate Syndrome')." Keynote Address at the Conference on Women and Sport. Western Illinois University, Macomb, Illinois. June 28, 1973.

INDEX